Education Law in Canada

GENERAL EDITOR

A. Wayne MacKay

Emond Montgomery's
EDUCATION LAW TITLES

Beyond the "Careful Parent":
Tort Liability in Education
A. Wayne MacKay and Gregory M. Dickinson

Student Rights and Responsibilities:
Attendance and Discipline
Robert G. Keel

Canada's Legal Revolution: Public Education,
the Charter, and Human Rights
Terri A. Sussel

Teachers and the Law:
A Practical Guide for Educators
A. Wayne MacKay and Lyle Sutherland

Education Law: News and Commentary
for Educators About Legal Issues in Canda
Executive editor: Robert G. Keel
Associate editors: Gregory M. Dickinson,
A. Wayne MacKay, and Terri A. Sussel

Education Law's Human Resources Reporter:
Digests of Relevant Employment Law Decisions
Executive editor: Robert G. Keel

Beyond the "Careful Parent"

TORT LIABILITY IN EDUCATION

A. Wayne MacKay

Gregory M. Dickinson

Printed in Canada.

Edited, designed, and typeset by WordsWorth Communications, Toronto.

Canadian Cataloguing in Publication Data

MacKay, A. Wayne, 1949–
    Beyond the "careful parent" : tort liability in education

(Education law in Canada series)
ISBN 0-920722-85-7

1. Liability for school accidents – Canada. 2. Tort liability of school districts – Canada. 3. Educational law and legislation – Canada.
    I. Dickinson,
G.M. (Gregory M.), 1947– . II. Title. III. Series.

KE1288.S3M32 1998   344.71'075   C98-931618-1
KF1309.M32 1998

To my late father, Alexander MacBeth MacKay, who served on school boards and was dedicated to the value of education.

A. Wayne MacKay

To my wife, Candace; my daughter, Nicole; and my mother, Joan, whose memory we all cherish.

Gregory M. Dickinson

Table of Contents

Preface

Beyond the "Careful Parent": Tort Liability in Education updates and expands the analysis of school tort liability begun by A. Wayne MacKay in the seminal work *Education Law in Canada*. It attempts to explain what is arguably the most fertile area of education litigation by organizing the discussion according to the teacher's rather than the lawyer's world. Although a degree of legal jargon is inescapable, we have attempted to minimize it and to present the material in a cognitive framework that will make sense to laypersons and resonate, in particular, with educators.

As longtime teachers of education law in undergraduate, graduate, and professional continuing education settings, we are keenly aware of the anxiety that the threat of liability engenders in teachers and school administrators—novice and veteran alike. Although it is fair to say that, of all of the areas of judicial involvement in educational policy and practice, tort liability is the one where courts are apt to show the least deference and tolerance for questionable conduct by educators, it is also true that much of the angst we have witnessed on the part of educators regarding their legal vulnerability is attributable to misleading information and impressions gleaned from professional folklore and mass media. We view this book therefore as very much a vehicle for continuing our teaching mission and ensuring the availability of an accurate portrayal of the topic of tort liability in schools. This book's raison d'etre, however, transcends the "teachers and the law" or the "teacher's manual" approach, providing instead a more comprehensive treatment of the issues and often including critical and analytical commentary thereon.

It has been more than a century since two mischievous English school boys clandestinely took a bottle of phosphorus from a locked cupboard at school and burned themselves. Their misadventure spawned what we commonly recognise as the landmark school negligence case, *Williams v. Eady*, in which Lord Esher articulated the durable "careful parent" test that courts continue to use to determine negligence on the part of someone under a legal duty of care toward a child. In 1998, however, as the title of our book implies, the question of liability for injury at school is so much more complex than what is suggested by Lord Esher's rudimentary concept. Hence our book explores the question of liability based also on the notion of teachers as experts practising their profession in a number of specialized settings, such as the regular classroom, gyms and playing fields, shops, labs, extraschool excursions, and so forth. It also considers the particular position of school trustees who, although personally liable for their conduct in some instances, are usually held to be automatically responsible in law simply by dint of the master-servant relationship between them and a teacher who is directly responsible for an injury to a student (so-called vicarious liability) or as occupiers of the premises where an accident occurs (so-called occupier's liability). We also expand the discussion to vicarious liability for intentional torts and begin to probe the evolving issues surrounding school board liability for teachers' sexual assault or abuse of students.

Our treatment of tort liability extends beyond cases of physical harm and considers the prospect of liability for intellectual harm, including failure to educate and negligent identification and placement of exceptional pupils. Our experience tells us that many members of the general public and, indeed, the educational community itself, are shocked to learn that this form of educational malpractice has rarely, if ever, been held to be actionable in court. We examine the legal and public policy reasons for the historical failure of such suits in the United States, Canada, and elsewhere and discuss whether opportunities may and should still exist for their eventual success in certain situations.

Tort law—the law that largely governs liability for school-related injuries—is almost exclusively based on the common law—that is, law made by judges in individual cases. The outcome of torts cases hinges a great deal on how a judge or jury interprets conflicting evidence and arcane legal concepts. Invariably, the individual biases and experiences of jury members and judges influence the meaning they give to evidence and how they apply legal tests. Cases are very much the product of both their time and their individual human participants. These simple realities make the study of cases a highly unpredictable business and help explain the sometimes apparently contradictory stances and outcomes across the cases we discuss. The challenge is to determine their degree of generalizability—for lawyers and jurists to determine their precedent value, and for educators to assist in developing sound risk-management policies and practices. Beyond these practical applications, however, many of the cases are intrinsically interesting and disclose much about how, as a society, we cope with difficult moral questions involving ultimate responsibility owed to vulnerable persons in a state-controlled environment. We hope that this book serves all these ends.

Gregory M. Dickinson
A. Wayne MacKay

Acknowledgments

I would like to acknowledge those people who assisted me with chapter 5 of the original *Education Law in Canada* (1984), which provided the foundation of this book. The contributions of the school administrators, teachers, and education law students with whom we have discussed these issues have been great. They helped to keep us grounded in the practical reality of the schools and the need to balance risk and caution in the process of education.

A. Wayne MacKay

I am grateful for the technical support and assistance I received from Stephanie Macleod, and for the financial support of the Division of Educational Policy Studies, Faculty of Education, the University of Western Ontario, which enabled me to use electronic databases in my research of the topics in this book. Finally, as always, I am thankful I have a family who value scholarship and who cheerfully indulge the occasional grumpiness and absent-mindedness that inevitably accompany the critical stages of any writing project of this magnitude. In this sense, the product is partly their accomplishment too.

Gregory M. Dickinson

Table of Cases

1

Introduction

One of the questions most frequently asked by teachers and school boards is, When can we be sued? The question does not indicate that school personnel are paranoid; rather, it is a recognition of the fact that most of the Canadian cases related to education have involved law suits against schools. On the whole, Canadian judges have been relatively lenient with respect to school personnel, although some commentators argue that tougher standards are now being imposed.[1] The increase in litigation has occurred largely because the target of a lawsuit is no longer the local community school but large incorporated school boards and faceless insurance companies. In times of economic restraint the number of accidents and the number of lawsuits are both likely to increase. Old or defective equipment is less likely to be replaced, fewer teacher's aides will be hired, and the number of teachers may decrease.

There is no simple answer to the question of when schools can be sued for a breach of duty leading to liability for damages. The range of litigious issues is as varied as human experience itself. Children are highly inventive in finding ways to be injured, and schools today provide an increasingly large array of potentially and even inherently dangerous activities and circumstances. Moreover, teachers, like parents, vary widely in their responses to situations of risk. Provincial education acts provide little guidance on the question of when schools can be sued, although the acts do set out certain relevant duties and standards.

The question of liability is largely governed by common law, or legal principles established by judges in cases. Therefore, this book will provide an overview of the considerable body of case law in the area of liability for accidents. While the overall perspective of this book is distinctly legal, the analysis is broken down into a number of subheadings representing topics that locate

---

[1] D.H. Rogers, "Educational Malpractice—Teachers and Standards of Care," in J. Balderson and J. Kolmes, eds., *Legal Issues in Canadian Education: Proceedings of the 1982 Canadian School Executive Conference* (Edmonton: Canadian School Executive, 1983), 125.

the legal principles within the educator's rather than the law-yer's world. First, however, we will introduce the theoretical legal framework of the law of torts, in general, and more particularly, of the law of negligence.

Torts and Civil Liability

Civil and Criminal Liability

"Tort" is derived from the Latin word *tortus*, meaning crooked or twisted. A tortious act is a civil and not a criminal wrong because it involves private rather than public harm. Criminal liability arises when a person engages in conduct that contravenes social standards as expressed by criminal laws. Civil liability arises when a person engages in conduct that results in harm to another private individual. These "private wrongs" are enforced by the person who suffers the harm, or someone acting on his or her behalf, in order to recover compensation for the loss. In some cases the same conduct can give rise to criminal and civil liability. For example, assaults in the form of corporal punishment can result in both criminal prosecution and civil action. The existence of Criminal Code provisions on negligence,[2] an essentially private law concept, also emphasizes the potential for overlap.

Definition

One of the most frequently quoted definitions of "tort" is that given by W.L. Prosser:

> Tort is a term applied to a miscellaneous and more or less unconnected group of civil wrongs, other than breach of contract, for which a court of law will afford a remedy in the form of an action for damages. The law of torts is concerned with the compensation of losses suffered by private individuals in their legally protected interests, through conduct of others which is regarded as socially unreasonable.[3]

---

[2] Criminal Code, RSC 1985, c. C-46, as amended (herein referred to as "the Code"), s. 219.

[3] W.L. Prosser, *Handbook of the Law of Torts*, 2d ed. (St Paul, MN: West Publishing Co., 1955), 1, as cited in P.F. Bargen, *The Legal Status of the Canadian Public School Pupil* (Toronto: Macmillan, 1961), 134-35, and S.G. McCurdy, *The Legal Status of the Canadian Teacher* (Toronto: Macmillan, 1968), 131.

Intentional and Unintentional Torts

The private wrongs defined as torts may be either intentional or unintentional in nature. An intentional tort is one about which it can be said that the wrongdoer intended to cause harm, as in the case of assaults, battery, or false imprisonment. Unintentional torts, usually referred to as negligence, occur when a person ought to have foreseen that his or her actions would cause harm. This book is primarily concerned with the concept of negligence.

In summary, a tort is not a crime. The category includes most civil wrongs with the exception of breach of contract. It is primarily a common law doctrine, although statutes can impose civil liability for their breach. However, breach of a statute is more likely to be viewed as evidence of negligence than as a separate tort.[4] Statutes may be used to define the appropriate standard of conduct or quantify the necessary degree of care. In general, a person will be liable in tort only if he or she intends to do harm to others or is negligent in that reasonable precautions are not taken to prevent foreseeable harm.

Negligence Law

The term "negligence" is a familiar one. It is clearly negligent to drive on the wrong side of the road or to give a loaded gun to a two-year-old child. A central concept of the law of negligence is that a person should be able to predict when his or her actions might create risks that could cause harm to others. Such risks should not be created; if they must be created, preventive measures should be taken to diminish the chances of harm to others. Both the potential victims and the risks themselves must be foreseeable before there will be liability for negligence. It is no defence to a claim of negligence to say that you did not foresee the harm if it is true that a reasonable person in the same circumstances would have foreseen it.

In simplified terms, legal liability for negligence depends on the existence of three elements: a duty of care, a breach of the standard of care, and damage or injury that results from the breach.

---

[4] See *Saskatchewan Wheat Pool v. Government of Canada* (1983), 45 NR 425 (SCC).

Duty of Care

Everyone has a duty to conduct himself or herself so as not to harm others. In order for liability to arise it is necessary that both the harm caused and the person injured should have been "reasonably foreseeable." The test often used by courts is whether a "reasonable person" would have foreseen the accident.

The eighteenth century English satirist A.P. Herbert provides us with a humorous description of the centrepiece of English common law, the "reasonable man":

> The Common Law of England has been laboriously built about a mythical figure—the figure of the "Reasonable Man." ... He is an ideal, a standard, the embodiment of all those qualities which we demand of the good citizen. ... The Reasonable Man is always thinking of others; prudence is his guide and "Safety First" ... is his rule of life. ... He is one who invariably looks where he is going, and is careful to examine the immediate foreground before he executes a leap or bound; who neither star-gazes nor is lost in meditation when approaching trap-doors or the margin of a dock; ... who never mounts a moving omnibus, and does not alight from any car while the train is in motion; ... and will inform himself of the history and habits of a dog before administering a caress; ... who never drives his ball till those in front of him have definitely vacated the putting-green; ... who never from one year's end to another makes an excessive demand on his wife, his neighbours, his servants, his ox, or his ass; ... who never swears, gambles or loses his temper; who uses nothing except in moderation, and even while he flogs his child is meditating only on the golden mean. Devoid, in short, of any human weakness, with not one single saving vice ... , as careful for his own safety as he is for that of others, this excellent but odious character ... stands like a monument in our Courts of Justice, vainly appealing to his fellow-citizens to order their lives after his own example.[5]

As Herbert implies, the concept of a "reasonable person" is a legal fiction, since there is probably no actual person who could be said to be completely "reasonable." Nonetheless, the question is not what the mythical reasonable person would do, or even what the majority of people would do; it is what the reasonable

---

[5] A.P. Herbert, *Uncommon Law* (London: Methuen & Co., 1935), 1-4.

person would do in the same circumstances, in the opinion of the presiding judge or jury, that in reality becomes the standard.

If it is foreseeable that someone might be harmed, it is necessary for a person to take whatever steps a reasonable or prudent person would take to avoid injury. It is important to note that this does not require a person to take steps to *eliminate* the possibility of harm, but only to take reasonable steps to *minimize* the risk of injury. For example, where an outdoor hockey rink is bordered by a pedestrian sidewalk, it is foreseeable that a pedestrian might be hit by a flying puck. The owner of the rink owes a duty to passing pedestrians to prevent injury from flying pucks. This duty probably does not require the owner to prohibit hockey games or completely enclose the rink. A reasonable person probably would erect boards and a screen, and this is the standard the owner must meet.

Teachers and school authorities have special duties of care imposed on them because of the nature of their work. They are entrusted with the heavy responsibility of caring for large numbers of young children. Some provincial education statutes impose additional duties on school personnel with respect to such matters as maintaining and supervising school premises, providing safe transportation, and attending to the safety and comfort of students. Those duties may be further clarified by regulations, school board bylaws, policy statements, and job descriptions. The exact nature of the duties varies somewhat from province to province, but the general thrust is similar across Canada.

If an express duty is imposed by statute, regulation, or even a school rule, then a court would consider a breach of the statute or rule in deciding whether an educator has been negligent. A breach of a school rule *per se* will not usually be considered negligent, but it can be an important factor in negligence. Breach of a statutory duty is a more serious matter. One of the first tasks of the prudent educator is to become informed about his or her duties, which expand or contract one's normal duty of care as a citizen.

Breach of the Standard of Care

The proper standard of care in negligence law varies according to the situation. In some instances it is defined exclusively by the common law; in others, it is defined partly by statute. For professionals, such as doctors or lawyers, a higher standard of competence is expected than for lay persons performing the same task.

The standard of care expected of school personnel is usually that of a "careful parent." School personnel are expected to use the same degree of caution that careful or prudent parents would use in the care of their own children. It should be noted that this duty is somewhat modified to take account of the fact that a teacher typically has charge of many more children than does a parent. In spite of the obvious problems in applying the careful-parent standard to the school setting, it is still the benchmark preferred by the judiciary. All attempts to move exclusively to the standard of the reasonable teacher, reasonable principal, or competent physical education instructor have failed. When accidents occur at school, school personnel will usually be liable in negligence only if their conduct falls below that expected of the careful parent.

Damage Resulting from Breach of the Standard of Care

The third element on which legal liability depends is the one that is least understood by the lay person. "Damage" is a legal term for physical injury, economic losses, or even nervous shock. Those damages that are legally recognized change over time. Unless some legally recognized damages have occurred, there can be no successful negligence action. Although giving a loaded gun to a two-year-old may in itself be negligent in the general use of that term, it will only be negligent in law if an injury occurs. Furthermore, the injury must result from the negligent act; there must be a causal connection.

It should be emphasized that the mere occurrence of an accident does not necessarily indicate negligence. If a group of students is taken on a field trip and one of them is hit by lightning, the supervising teacher will be found negligent only if he or she caused the accident in some way—for example, by making the student stand under a tree, or by failing to warn the student about the dangers of being near a solitary tree in an electrical storm. Note that a person can be negligent by an act of omission as well as commission.

The basic principle underlying civil actions for damages is that the innocent party should be compensated for any loss caused by the wrongdoer. If there is no injury or damage, there can be no compensation and therefore no liability. If a teacher is negligent and exposes a student to an unreasonable risk of harm, he or she will not be liable if the student is fortunate enough to avoid harm.

Where injury does occur, however, the negligent conduct must be its cause. For example, a teacher may be negligent in not providing adequate supervision in the classroom. However, if a student is struck and injured by another student during the teacher's absence, there will be no liability unless the court is satisfied that proper supervision would have prevented the harm. Therefore, a person might behave in a manner that most people would term negligent, but if the behaviour is not the cause of the resulting loss or injury, or if no injury or loss occurs, then there can be no negligence in a legal sense.

It is possible that the injured person may have contributed to his or her injury by not taking reasonable steps to avoid harm. In such a case the injured person is said to have been "contributorily negligent," and must bear some of his or her own loss. This is discussed in more detail in chapter 4. One of the critical questions in all negligence cases is who should bear the loss. In practical terms it often involves determining which insurance company should compensate the victim for the loss. Of course, there is a direct effect on the parties because insurance premiums normally rise as a result of an accident. Furthermore, not all parents or even all teachers are adequately insured, although most school boards are.

2

Teacher Liability for Accidents

The Teacher–Student Relationship

The proper supervision of students is one of a teacher's major duties. As discussed in chapter 1, teachers' duties with respect to the safety of the students under their care arise in part from statutes, regulations, and policies, but the teacher–student relationship itself also produces a common law duty of care. It is clear that this legal relationship is not restricted to cases where students are under the age of majority. Therefore, where a 19-year-old student fell off a mountain during a field trip, the board and supervising teacher were held liable for negligent supervision.[1] The court rejected the contention that the student's adulthood vitiated the student–teacher relationship creating a legal duty of care. In any event, the court observed, a legal duty of care is created in any proximate relationship where reasonable people would expect that one of the persons in the relationship would take reasonable care not to expose the other to foreseeable and unreasonable risk of accident and injury.[2]

The specific legal duty of care teachers owe their pupils arises from an application of the *in loco parentis* doctrine. The idea that a school or its teachers are given a temporary delegation of parental authority made some sense in the English residential school or the small one-room school, but it is of little value in the modern public school.[3] Nonetheless, the explanation of teachers' tort liability in terms of the doctrine of *in loco parentis*, as in cases such as *Ramsay v. Larsen*,[4] has survived to this day. Statutory enactments have

---

[1] *Bain v. Calgary Board of Education* (1993), 14 Alta. LR (3d) 319 (QB).

[2] See Lord Atkin's remarks about the legal concept of "neighbours," in *Donoghue v. Stevenson*, [1932] AC 562.

[3] *MacDonald's Tutor v. County Council of Inverness*, [1937] SC 69, at 77 (Inner House), per Lord MacKay.

[4] *Ramsay v. Larsen* (1964), ALR 1121 (Aust. HC).

helped to clarify both the duty and the standard of care, but the common law roots of the relationship are still important.

Provincial education statutes impose various duties on teachers in addition to the duty to teach diligently. The most important of these in the context of teacher liability is the duty to maintain order and discipline.[5] There is generally also a duty imposed on the school board to supervise the school and premises. This duty is usually delegated to the principals and teaching staff by the school board.

The Careful-Parent Rule

The Rule

It is a well-established legal principle that teachers are expected to use the same degree of care with respect to their students as prudent or careful parents would use with their own children. The case most often referred to as the origin of this rule is *Williams v. Eady*.[6] In that case, the plaintiff was injured when phosphorus used to paint cricket balls exploded while being handled by another student. The schoolmaster was held liable for failure to keep the dangerous substance in a place where the pupils would not have access to it. In his decision, Lord Esher made the following statement:

> [T]he schoolmaster was bound to take such care of his boys as a careful father would take of his boys, and there could be no better definition of the duty of a schoolmaster. Then he was bound to take notice of the ordinary nature of young boys, their tendency to do mischievous acts, their propensity to meddle with anything that came in their way.[7]

The finding of negligence on the particular facts of *Williams v. Eady* sets a high standard of care for teachers. The jury did not reject the assertion that the teacher had locked the phosphorus in an appropriate room and that the mischievous boys had obtained the key by stealth. Lord Esher, however, seemed to accept the view that the phosphorus was left within the reach of the boys. In any case, the accident occurred only after a lighted match

---

[5] Education Act, SNS 1995-96, c. 1. s. 74(b); Education Act, RSO 1990, c. E.2, s. 264(l)(e); and Public Schools Act, RSM 1987, c. P-250, s. 96(c) are but three examples.

[6] *Williams v. Eady* (1894), 10 TLR 41 (CA).

[7] Ibid., at 42.

was placed in the bottle and the bottle was shaken. The court held that the negligence of the teacher had caused the accident.

Reservations

The careful-parent test has come under fire as a paternalistic and outmoded standard that bears little relation to the actual school situation of today.[8] Described as an "elastic yardstick," the test has also been criticized for offering little real guidance to the court because it sets a standard so flexible that judges can bend it any way that they desire.[9] Laura Hoyano argues that one of the major problems with the careful-parent test is that it places an unfairly high standard on school officials.[10] As a matter of logic this is true, but as a matter of fact courts have been reluctant to find that teachers are in breach of their duties. This suggests that the flexibility of the rule, and not its harshness, is the major source of concern. Moreover, in some instances, it is arguable whether a parentally based test would be strict enough—for example, where injuries result from mishaps in shops, gymnasia, laboratories, or other places where professional expertise should be expected of a supervisor.

One of the most obvious contrasts between a parent's and a teacher's situation is the large number of children for which the teacher is responsible. One judge has suggested that the effect of the increased numbers is to place a higher standard of care on the teacher, because an increase in unruly behaviour can be expected from a group of children.[11] More often, courts have emphasized the need to be realistic about the degree of supervision that is reasonable where large numbers of children are concerned. *Ricketts v. Erith Borough Council* provides a clear articulation of this viewpoint:

> [I]n considering the facts of a case like this, one has to visualize a parent with a very large family, because fifty children playing about in a yard is, of course, a different thing from four or five children playing together in a garden.[12]

---

[8] L.C.H. Hoyano, "The Prudent Parent: The Elusive Standard of Care" (1984), *University of British Columbia Law Review* 18, provides an excellent critique of the careful-parent rule.

[9] See R.L. Lamb, *Legal Liability of School Boards and Teachers for Accidents* (Ottawa: Canadian Teachers' Federation, 1959), 31.

[10] Supra note 8.

[11] See *Lyes v. Middlesex County Council* (1962), 61 LGR 443, at 446 (QB).

[12] *Ricketts v. Erith Borough Council*, [1943] 2 All ER 629, at 631 (KB).

In *Board of Education of Toronto and Hunt v. Higgs*,[13] Ritchie J conceded that the careful-parent test applied to the situation of the individual teacher, but felt it had less significance when applied to a school in general. It is thus less clear that the test for school board liability is always that of the careful parent. When a school sets up a system of supervision, it is responding to the large number of students under its care and not acting like a parent at all. In *McKay v. Board of Govan School Unit No. 29 Saskatchewan*,[14] Ritchie J expressed doubts that the careful-parent rule was universally applicable, even to teachers. Other judges have held that reference to the careful parent adds nothing to the normal requirements of reasonable care.[15]

The Rule Affirmed

The judicial reservations described above are exceptions to the general adoption of the careful-parent rule as a doctrine of universal application. A decision of the Supreme Court of Canada emphasizes this point. McIntyre J noted that the careful-parent test, as stated in *Williams v. Eady*, must be qualified in modern times. In *Myers et al. v. Peel County Board of Education et al.*, he outlined factors that must now be added to the careful-parent rule:

> It is not, however, a standard that can be applied in the same manner and to the same extent in every case. Its application will vary from case to case and will depend upon the number of students being supervised at any given time, the nature of the exercise or activity in progress, the age and the degree of skill and training which the students may have received in connection with such activity, the nature and condition of the equipment in use at the time, the competency and capacity of the students involved, and a host of other matters which may be widely varied but which, in a given case, may affect the application of the careful parent-standard to the conduct of the school authority in the circumstances.[16]

---

[13] *Board of Education of Toronto and Hunt v. Higgs* (1959), 22 DLR (2d) 49, at 55 (SCC).

[14] *McKay v. Board of Govan School Unit No. 29 Saskatchewan* (1968), 64 WWR 301, at 304 (SCC).

[15] See, for example, *Dyer v. Board of School Commissioners of Halifax* (1956), 2 DLR (2d) 394, at 399 (NS SC), per MacDonald J.

[16] *Myers et al. v. Peel County Board of Education et al.* (1981), 17 CCLT 269, at 279 (SCC).

The Need for Change

McIntyre J's extensive list of qualifications raises the legitimate question whether there is anything left of the original careful-parent test. As Hoyano suggests, the standard may have become a "rubber ruler" or an "elastic yardstick."[17] She argues that a more meaningful standard would be that of the reasonable and competent instructor. Such a standard would promote greater predictability in school negligence cases and impose some order on the chaotic collection of individual cases that now exist. We agree with Hoyano—the careful-parent rule should be abandoned as a doctrine that has outlived its usefulness. Unfortunately, this is not the current state of the law. There is scarcely a school negligence case that does not refer to *Williams v. Eady* and adopt the careful-parent rule as the appropriate standard of care; a century after its creation, the rule is alive and well in Canada.

Judicial attempts to shore up the careful-parent test, while conceding that it is not always entirely appropriate, have led to some rather confusing dicta. A particularly notable example occurs in *Thomas v. Board of Education of the City of Hamilton*.[18] In this case, discussed in more detail below,[19] a student was seriously injured during a football game as a result of the alleged negligence of his coaches. The standard of care applied by the court was the careful-parent test, adjusted by the circumstances to take into account the defendant coaches' expertise, which the court conceded was not the sort generally possessed by parents. It appears that the court assumed that in some cases some acts of alleged negligence need to be measured against a parental standard, while others, involving more specialized knowledge, training, or skill necessarily need to be gauged by professional criteria. Given the Court of Appeal's approach in *Thomas*, one might reasonably expect many school accident cases to involve the application of two different standards.

Application of the Careful-Parent Rule

While the duties placed on teachers to avoid harm befalling their students are constant, the standard that is required varies

---

[17] Supra note 8.

[18] *Thomas v. Board of Education of the City of Hamilton* (1994), 20 OR (3d) 598 (CA).

[19] See, in particular, the discussion of the case in the text accompanying note 100, infra.

depending on the circumstances. Relevant circumstances include the following:

- the age of the student or students;

- the nature of the activity [is it inherently dangerous or does it contain only an element of danger?];

- the amount of instruction received by the student;

- the student's general awareness [of risks involved];

- the approved general practice;

- the foreseeable risk of danger; [and]

- previous accidents in similar circumstances.[20]

These are only a few of the relevant factors. The facts of the case are crucial in any determination of negligence.

Before considering the wide range of situations in which teachers typically work, it is important to note a dynamic tension that pervades all aspects of a teacher's duties. On the one hand, a teacher must supervise and protect the students within his or her charge; this demands a certain degree of paternalism. On the other hand, one of the teacher's most important educational goals is to produce independent and self-reliant children who are capable of looking after themselves. In this respect the teacher does face the same dilemma as the parent—How do you protect a child from the many risks of the outside world without smothering his or her inherent spirit of adventure and need for independence? There is no simple answer, and both parent and teacher must walk the fine line between sheltering a child and allowing him or her to learn by making mistakes. As the child grows older, the focus must shift from protection to independence. This process must begin when the child is young, with teachers and parents deciding which decisions can reasonably be left to the child.[21] The teacher's position is more vulnerable than the parent's—it is the teacher who is more likely to be sued for a miscalculation.

---

[20] A.M. Thomas, *Accidents Will Happen: An Inquiry into the Legal Liability of Teachers and School Boards* (Toronto: OISE Press, 1976), 42. According to Thomas's review of the decided cases, these factors were the primary ones that influenced the courts in determining that there was a breach of the proper standard of supervision.

[21] See *Jeffrey v. London County Council* (1954), 119 JP 45 (QB). This case held that it was reasonable to leave a 5-year-old child unsupervised in the playground as a valid means of promoting the "sturdy independence of children."

In *Suckling v. Essex County Council*,[22] a student was injured by a knife removed from an unlocked cupboard in a handicraft class. The accident occurred during horseplay that broke out in the teacher's absence. The ruling provides an interesting contrast to *Williams v. Eady*, which involved a similar fact situation. Vaisey J, in deciding in favour of the defendant school authorities, made the following comments:

> It seems to me that if I were to hold that every school with small children was committing an actionable wrong in leaving unlocked such implements as these scorer knives I would be putting an altogether excessive burden on educational establishments. Not only would it be difficult for them to be conducted in a successful and reasonable manner but it would run the risk of turning these children into votaries of the principle of safety first. It is better that a boy should break his neck than allow other people to break his spirit.[23]

Horseplay with knives may not be the kind of youthful spirit that should be promoted, but the general point of the judgment is well taken. The age of the student concerned is important, and the manifestation of "spirit" that will be tolerated changes with time and the personalities involved. Some commentators lament the line of paternalistic jurisprudence originating with *Williams v. Eady* and criticize the courts for placing an unfair burden on supervising teachers and sending the wrong message to children about the need to be responsible for their own actions. According to W.H. Giles, for example:

> [T]he courts must not be ignorant or overprotective, and at once make an ass of the law, and destroy the schools. We must remember that children need to grow, and teachers need to let them grow. Teachers are not negligent when they do what is necessary in order to enable the children to grow. It must be remembered that, while it is normal for grandparents to be overprotective, it is also destructive.
>
> It is said by some that the real basis for liability has not increased; the author submits that this is untrue. ... The duty of care at the time of *Donoghue and Stevenson*, [1932] AC 562 (HL), was that of a limited character. It is submitted that,

---

[22] *Suckling v. Essex County Council* (January 27, 1955), *The Times* (London), reproduced in G.R. Barrell, *Legal Cases for Teachers* (London: Methuen, 1970), 245.

[23] Ibid., at 245.

since that time, judges have expanded those reasonable rules into a complete compensation system designed to take away a person's responsibility for his or her own wrongdoing, and to impose it on others. ... Making innocents liable is immoral and tends to bring the judicial system into contempt. The author submits that our whole society has been undermined in this area by the courts in having permitted this to happen. The removal of swings from children's playgrounds is but the most obvious sign. It is up to the courts to return the swings, the dances, the ski trips, the playground[s], etc., to the children by ensuring that those who engage in wrongdoing, assume the responsibility for their own acts.[24]

The philosophy espoused by Giles and reflected in *Suckling* is not, however, representative of prevailing judicial attitudes. Lord Esher's sentiments in *Williams v. Eady* are clearly echoed in the Supreme Court of Canada's judgment in *Myers v. Peel County Board of Education et al.*, where McIntyre J stated:

The respondent [teacher] should have anticipated reckless behaviour from at least some of the young boys sent off by themselves to work on gymnastic equipment. The evidence revealed that it was a recurring problem to keep students from attempting gymnastic exercises without spotters and the proclivity of young boys of high school age to act recklessly in disregard, if not in actual defiance, of authority is, as was pointed out by Blair JA, in dissent in the Court of Appeal, well known.[25]

Recently, in *Kowalchuk v. Middlesex County Board of Education*,[26] where a 12-year-old boy broke his arm after flipping off a high-jump mat that students had been told to stay off, Gautreau J adopted a similar measure of paternalism when he observed:

On the question of reasonable anticipation a school board must take into account the unpredictable and adventuresome nature of young people in finding ways to entertain themselves including those involving risks.[27]

The study of educators' liability for accidents, thus reveals a dynamic tension between accountability for children's safety and

---

[24] W.H. Giles, *Schools and Students* (Toronto: Carswell, 1988), 100-1.

[25] Supra note 16, at 282.

[26] *Kowalchuk v. Middlesex County Board of Education*, [1991] OJ no. 1122 (Gen. Div.), aff'd. [1994] OJ no. 1103 (CA).

[27] Ibid., [1991] OJ no. 1122, at 8.

accountability for their education and overall development. Teachers face the constant challenge of striking a reasonable balance between protecting students and giving them enough rein to develop their independence and sense of risk taking.[28]

The Classroom

Most school-related accidents occur in hallways, on playgrounds, or on field trips. Although teachers spend most of their time in the classroom, they are least often sued for their actions or inactions there. Physical education and shop teachers are the principal exceptions to this generalization—they do attract lawsuits while performing the main task for which they are employed. Their liability is discussed later in this chapter.

A teacher has the duty to supervise students in the classroom, but this apparently does not mean constant supervision. In a 1983 Ontario case, *McCue et al. v. Board of Education for Etobicoke*,[29] a student's eye was injured when another student fired a paper clip from an elastic band during the teacher's absence from the classroom. The court chose to find no liability on the teacher's part since, in the court's view, the incident was not foreseeable. Similarly, when a teacher left her special-education class unattended and one student was injured by another in a scuffle, the court said that the teacher's absence was not negligence.[30] The US court took note of the fact that the teacher was only absent for five minutes and that she had instructed a neighbouring teacher to supervise the class. This neighbouring teacher heard only the usual noise of a play period in the adjoining room.

In another US case, where a grade 4 student was accidentally hit and injured by another student when the teacher left the room during calisthenics, the teacher was not found liable.[31] As in *McCue*, the court stated that the injury was not a reasonably foreseeable result of the teacher's absence and was not caused by

---

[28] See A. van Holst and G. Dickinson, "Present Practices Regarding the Use of Protective Floor Covering for Climbing Apparatus" (September-October 1988), *Canadian Association for Health, Physical Education and Recreation Journal* 7.

[29] An unreported decision of Carruthers J, September 24, 1982 (Ont. SC), summarized in J. Anderson, "Student Responsibility for Injury to Other Student" (1983), vol. 3, no. 4 *Canadian School Executive* 30. See also the discussion of the case in chapter 5, below.

[30] *McDonald v. Terrebonne Parish School Board*, 253 So. 2d 558 (La. CA 1971).

[31] *Segerman v. Jones*, 259 A2d 794 (Md. CA 1969).

it, but rather by the other student. This conclusion is surprising, since one would expect that a grade 4 class doing exercises as directed by a recording should be supervised. The court concluded that the accident would have occurred whether or not the teacher was there; thus, even if the teacher were negligent, there was no causal connection. This might be dubbed the defence of teacher impotence.[32]

Such reasoning appears to disregard the deterrent value of a teacher's presence. Paradoxically, other courts have linked liability to the teacher's absence, which the courts ruled would have deterred students from wrongful or dangerous conduct.[33] There seems to be no reliable way to predict whether a court will view teachers as effective deterrents and thus whether their absence will amount to negligence causing the injuries in question. The safe course of action is, of course, to err on the side of caution, to assume that the courts view teachers as effective deterrents, and to avoid leaving students unattended. The reasons for any absence, its duration, the type of accident, and the nature of the class are all factors that could lead to a finding of negligence in a Canadian court. Indeed, as we shall see below, a chemistry teacher who left his class for a moment during an experiment was held negligent and liable for injuries to a student whose experiment blew up in her face.[34]

Playgrounds and Outside

When a child is injured outside the classroom, the question arises whether an adequate system of supervision was in place and, if so, whether the teachers responsible for supervision adequately performed their task. If the inadequacy of the system was the cause of the accident, then the principal or other person responsible for supervision of school premises will be liable.[35] Of course, if his or her failure to provide proper supervision results in an injury to a student, the teacher will be liable.

---

[32] See *Board of Education of Toronto and Hunt v. Higgs*, supra note 13.

[33] *Myers v. Peel County Board of Education*, supra note 16.

[34] *James v. River East, School Division No. 9*, [1976] 2 WWR 577 (Man. CA).

[35] Lamb, supra note 9, at 120, suggests that the principal of a school has a greater legal liability than a regular teacher. Added duties are frequently imposed by school board bylaws or policy statements.

The Supreme Court of Canada in *Board of Education for the City of Toronto v. Higgs*[36] held that there was no liability where a bully injured another student—the court was not satisfied that increased supervision would have prevented the injury. While the court indicated that the known mischievous tendencies of the bully increased the range of foreseeable risks, it was silent as to whether teachers have a duty to inform themselves of the proclivities of the students under their supervision. The effect of more information would often be to expand the range of foreseeable risks.[37] This issue has serious implications where student criminal offenders are involved, and the law, which formerly impeded educators' access to information about the criminal activities of young persons, was amended in 1995 to facilitate obtaining such information where school safety is at risk.[38]

After noting that it was the responsibility of the principal to ensure an adequate system of supervision, the court in *Higgs* held that the standard to be expected was not that of a careful parent but that of a "prudent school principal." Whether this imposes a higher or lower standard than the careful-parent rule is unclear, but it may permit a principal to rely on the general practice of other principals in avoiding liability for inadequate supervision. In some cases a higher standard will be imposed on the principal by statutes, regulations, or school board policies.

In *Higgs*, the student was injured when he fell on ice during recess. The critical question was whether the system of supervision was adequate. There were 750 students in the school, and the playground measured 400 feet by 250 feet. On the day in question, the four teachers on supervision duty were strategically located at the corners of the playground. The court was inclined to the view that this was an adequate system of supervision even in the more dangerous winter conditions. It did not have to determine this point, however, as it held that there was no causal connection between the number of supervisors and the accident. The supervising teachers responded quickly to the accident and there was no indication that more supervisors would

---

[36] Supra note 13.

[37] *McLaughlin v. Holy Cross High School*, 521 NYS (2d) 744 (CA 1987).

[38] See the Young Offenders Act, RSC 1985, c. Y-1, s. 38, as amended by SC 1995, c. 19, s. 27. See also R. Keel, *The Rights and Responsibilities of Students: Attendance and Discipline* (Toronto: Emond Montgomery, forthcoming).

have prevented it. In fact, a supervising teacher had been standing within 30 to 40 feet of the incident.

A teacher will not be liable for inadequate supervision of school grounds unless it can be shown that he or she should have seen the incident in sufficient time to prevent the injury. Therefore, in *Dyer*, when a small group of boys out of several hundred students was tossing acorns, there was no liability on the four supervising teachers for failing to see and stop this conduct before one of the boys was hit in the eye.[39] It was also significant that the acorns were brought onto the school grounds by the boys and that the throwing of them was of brief duration. After *Dyer*, on the first day of school, the principal made it a practice to announce his rule against throwing any objects on the school grounds. Such a practice makes it easy to verify the exact date of the announcement if the need arises. The safest course is to distribute a written statement of school rules to teachers, parents, and, where appropriate, the students themselves. Not only will this be useful evidence in a negligence case, but it may also realize the more important objective of preventing accidents in the schools.

The *Higgs* and *Dyer* decisions, however, should not be read as providing any kind of blanket immunity against liablity for schoolyard accidents. Other courts have not been loath to impose liability in the right set of circumstances. For example, in *Hentze v. Board of School Trustees of School District No. 72*,[40] liability was imposed when a student was injured during a bout of roughhousing with some older boys during the lunch hour recess. While recognizing the Supreme Court of Canada's admonition in *Higgs* that the law does not require that students be kept under supervision at all times, the court noted that the application of the standard of care—that of the reasonably careful and prudent parent—depended on the nature and size of the area under supervision, the number of students and their ages, and the type of activities underway. The court found that the playfighting in question had gone on for several minutes and that if the supervising teacher had been carrying out reasonable supervision, she would have noticed the activity and put an end to it before the injury occurred.

---

[39] *Dyer v. Board of School Commissioners of Halifax*, supra note 15.

[40] *Hentze v. Board of School Trustees of School District No. 72* (1994), 49 BCAC 241 (CA).

The court's use of the board's own policies regarding schoolyard supervision is noteworthy. These policies identified safety in the yard as a prime concern. In particular, they outlawed playfighting and similar activities and obligated teachers to intervene immediately upon seeing such conduct. Moreover, it was contrary to the school's policy for younger children to play with older children because of a perceived increased risk of injury to the younger children. As a matter of law, it is clear that school boards and schools cannot establish a standard of care by drafting policies reflecting a level of conduct below that expected of a reasonably prudent parent. On the other hand, *Hentze* illustrates how failure to follow board or school policies may, at least, colour a case and strengthen a plaintiff's claim.

Liability for negligent schoolyard supervision was imposed also in *Kowalchuk v. Middlesex County Board of Education*,[41] where a 12-year-old boy broke his arm in three places after being catapulted off a high-jump mat and landing awkwardly. A group of students had been in the habit of using the mat for a game wherein a smaller boy would stand on one end of the mat while heavier boys would jump on the other end, setting up a wave motion that would catapult the smaller boy into the air. Teachers knew about this horseplay; in fact, the teacher in charge of the mat had told the boys not to play on it.

The court found that on the day of the accident there were only two teachers on yard duty supervising some 200 students and at the time of the accident they were both positioned so that their view of the senior yard (the site of the accident) was obscured. While the court recognized that the law did not require constant supervision, it held that teachers must nevertheless recognize the "unpredictable and adventuresome" nature of young people and their inventive ways of amusing themselves.[42] In the court's view, the mat had provided an attraction to the students. The board's duty was to either supervise its use or remove it—certainly the latter was easy to do. It was not sufficient for a teacher simply to order students not to use the mat; teachers must acknowledge that students do not always follow orders. The influence of McIntyre J's comments in *Myers* is obvious.

---

[41] Supra note 26.

[42] See *Kowalchuk*, supra note 26, where the students had invented a game involving a dangerous configuration of gymnastics equipment.

The court also noted the general tort principle that while the injury had to be foreseeable in order to find liability, the precise activity causing the injury or the sort of injury itself did not have to be foreseeable. It was enough that it was foreseeable that play of this general sort would lead to a possibility of injury of some kind. The court found the school board 80 percent liable and the student–plaintiff 20 percent responsible through his contributory negligence. Because of the permanent scarring that resulted, general damages were set at $36,000.

The *Kowalchuk* decision has been criticized on a number of grounds.[43] First, it seems paradoxical for the court to recognize that young boys' games are "unpredictable" and, at the same time, to hold that the events in the case were foreseeable. Second, the decision is said to be flawed for applying the wrong test for foreseeability—namely, the court found the injury foreseeable since there had been a possibility of injury arising from playing on the mat. The correct test, the critics allege, is whether the risk is foreseeable on a balance of probability. If by this the critics mean that to be foreseeable the occurrence of an event must be more probable than not, they are in error. As Fleming puts it:

> [T]he chance of injury need not attain comparative *probability*; the test of "more probable than not" we use to establish that a certain event has happened in the past, not whether it is fraught with danger in the future. In fact, the test has become so "undemanding" that the injury need not even be "likely." All that is required is that the risk be "real" in the sense that a reasonable person would not "brush it aside as far-fetched" or fanciful.[44]

Finally, the degree of contributory negligence (20 percent) assessed by the court in *Kowalchuk* has been criticized insofar as it equals that assessed in *Myers*, where the activity was inherently rather than merely potentially dangerous, encouraged by the teacher and conducted in an unsupervised area to which the student had been sent. The critics of the *Kowalchuk* decision suggest that it has "greatly expanded" the standard of care to be exercised by school boards. We believe, however, that these critics

---

[43] See "Liability for Abuse of Inherently Harmless Equipment" (November 1991), 3 *EduLaw for Canadian Schools* 19, at 20.

[44] J.G. Fleming, *The Law of Torts*, 7th ed. (Sydney: The Law Book Company, 1987), 105. See also *Brown v. Essex County Roman Catholic Separate School Board*, [1990] OJ no. 1455 (HCJ).

pay too little attention to some of the facts that negatively colour this case—the lack of a deterrent supervisor in the area to enforce the order not to play on the mats and the ease with which the mat could have been removed. Moreover, it is hard to see how foreseeability is even an issue when orders not to play on the mat were given prior to the accident.

In *Catherwood v. Board of School Trustees, School District No. 22 (Vernon),*[45] the BC Supreme Court showed leniency to two teachers who were supervising a baseball game involving 25 students. During the game, one of the students climbed a tree while waiting to bat. His antics were witnessed by a number of students, one of whom also climbed a tree. The second student slipped and fell about 15 feet to the ground, fracturing his wrist. Neither of the teachers, who were themselves playing in the game, saw either of the students climb the trees. Apparently less accepting of the reckless proclivities of adolescent boys than McIntyre J had been in *Myers* and Lord Esher in *Williams v. Eady*, the court in *Catherwood* ruled that the teachers could not have anticipated that a 16-year-old student would climb a tree.

Accidents, of course, occur in settings other than the playground. *Moffatt v. Dufferin County Board of Education*[46] provides an example. A 13-year-old boy was injured while helping the school janitor move a piano. The teacher had sent the boy to assist the janitor without inquiring about the exact nature of the task. This conduct was held to be consistent with the standard that would be observed by the careful parent, and no liability was imposed on the teacher.

Teachers can incur legal liability by assigning hazardous homework, banishing a student from the classroom, or sending him on an ill-fated errand.[47] Accidents are, of course, more likely to happen outside the classroom because the situation is less controlled.

Some cases have considered the nature and extent of the duty to supervise the hallways of schools. *Beharrell v. School District No. 34*[48] concerned a claim for damages against a school district

---

[45] *Catherwood v. Board of School Trustees, School District No. 22 (Vernon)*, [1996] BCJ no. 1373 (SC).

[46] *Moffatt v. Dufferin County Board of Education*, [1973] 1 OR 351 (CA).

[47] W.P. Hagenau, "Penumbras of Care Beyond the Schoolhouse Gate" (1980), 9 *Journal of Law and Education* 201.

[48] *Beharrell v. School District No. 34*, [1988] BCJ no. 3046 (SC).

by a grade 8 student who was injured in an incident in the corridor of his school. During the lunch break, while he was walking down the corridor, the plaintiff was jeered and pointed at by a group of students, one or more of whom grabbed his ankle, causing him to tumble onto his face. Consequently, the plaintiff injured his elbow and broke his glasses. When he subsequently sought assistance, the injured student had to walk up and down the corridors before encountering any teachers.

The evidence disclosed that it was normal practice for teachers to supervise the corridors during lunch break. According to the system in place, it was the responsibility of the supervising teachers to check the stairwells, hallways and washrooms and to watch for abnormal behaviour. The court found that there had been no teacher in the vicinity of the incident on the day in question. In passing, it is worth noting that the court had no choice but to accept the plaintiff's version of the facts regarding the proximity of teachers to the incident, because the defendant's only witness, the vice-principal, "recalled very little about this incident." This underscores the need for administrators and teachers involved in incidents with potential for litigation, to make careful and complete records of the events immediately after they occur. Evidentiary rules permit witnesses to use such records to refresh their memories.

The court ruled that the board had foreseen the need for supervision and had put in place a reasonable system to carry it out. On the day in question, however, the teachers had been "less than vigilant" in effecting the system and, therefore, the duty to supervise had been breached. The court then considered whether the plaintiff's injuries were caused by the defendant's negligent conduct. Several facts were found to be relevant to this issue—the hallway where the incident occurred was crowded; there was no shouting or anything else that would have attracted the attention of someone who was even close by; there was no history of violence in the hallways indicating a need for greater supervision; and the entire incident was brief, the tripping itself over in an instant.

Employing reasoning very like that of the Supreme Court in *Higgs*—though, remarkably, *Higgs* was not cited—the court found that there was no causal link between the breach of duty and the plaintiff's injuries:

> I have difficulty in concluding on balance that the presence of a supervisor would have made any difference, either from the point of view of the supervisor physically stepping in to pre-

vent the assault, or in the supervisor deferring [sic] its occurrence by virtue of being present. In fact, it is unlikely that
anyone, except perhaps the boy or boys who actually tripped
the plaintiff, could reasonably have anticipated that this would
be the consequence of the low-key teasing or taunting that
was directed towards the plaintiff at that time.[49]

Hallway supervision was also an issue in *Walsh v. Buchanan*,[50]
where a 19-year-old student was seriously injured in a hallway
fight with another student of the same age. Having been ejected
earlier from a floor hockey game for fighting, the two students
met coincidentally in the hall and began to punch each other. The
fight resulted in physical and emotional injuries to one of the
students. In his lawsuit against the other student and the school
authorities, the student-plaintiff alleged negligent supervision of
the hallways. In dismissing this part of the plaintiff's claim, the
court found the supervision reasonable and adequate under the
circumstances. Prudent parents of 19-year-olds would not think
it necessary to provide constant supervision of students who are
legally adults. Moreover, the court held that such a serious fight
was not reasonably foreseeable given that the vice-principal had
reprimanded the students for their earlier skirmish, threatened
them with suspension, and, most important, each student seemed
to heed the reprimand and to show no sign of continuing anger.

While the system of hallway supervision was found adequate
in these cases, it is worth emphasizing that reasonable foreseeability determines the nature and intensity of any supervision
system. The history of fighting and violence in a given school will
dictate the required standard of supervision—that is, it is a standard capable of shifting from time to time and place to place as
circumstances change. Therefore, boards and principals should
constantly monitor the level of risk associated with the use of
school hallways and other areas, such as washrooms, with a view
to establishing appropriate supervision policies. It is conceivable
that a history of hallway and schoolyard violence in a particular
school could elevate the foreseeability of risk sufficiently to require the installation of video surveillance equipment in the school
in order to discharge the board's duty of care, especially considering the logistical problems involved in patrolling the halls and
environs of a large school.

---

[49] Ibid., at 9-10.
[50] *Walsh v. Buchanan*, [1995] OJ no. 64 (Gen. Div.).

Before School Begins

In some provinces, education legislation prescribes rules governing the opening of school premises. For example, section 3(7) of
regulation 298 under Ontario's Education Act provides that a school
board "shall determine the period of time during each school day
when its school buildings and playgrounds shall be open to its
pupils, but in every case ... [they] shall be open to pupils during
the period beginning fifteen minutes before classes begin ... and
ending fifteen minutes after classes end for the day." It seems
reasonable to conclude that the school board's common law duty
to supervise its grounds would apply at least during the times
when the grounds are to be open pursuant to legislation. It should
be noted, however, that such legislation will probably be viewed
as providing minimal rules—that is, a common law obligation to
supervise students habitually arriving early probably exists, especially where the school appears to acquiesce in the practice.

Where students habitually arrive at school early, whoever has
a duty to provide supervision of school grounds during school
hours probably must ensure that such supervision is also provided before school begins. This is usually the principal or other
administrator rather than the individual teacher. When a student was injured prior to school by a paper clip shot from an
elastic band, the principal was said to have been negligent in
failing to provide an adequate system of supervision and failing
to set rules for the students.[51] The court noted that because the
students were expected to arrive early the principal's responsibility arose before classes began.

A duty may arise even though school board policies do not
expressly require pre-school supervision, because once the students are at school they are beyond parental protection and control. In addition, by permitting the students to arrive early the
teacher–student relationship is created and the associated responsibilities are assumed by the teacher. These conclusions were
reached by an Australian court in *Geyer v. Downs*,[52] where an 8-
year-old student was injured when playing, unsupervised, on the
school grounds before school. Although teachers will rarely be
responsible for providing a system of supervision, they may be
liable if they are assigned to supervise and are negligent in so

---

[51] *Titus v. Lindberg*, 38 ALR 3d 818 (NJ SC 1967).

[52] *Geyer v. Downs* (1977), 17 ALR 408 (Aust. CA).

doing. The major responsibility for pre-school supervision appears to rest with the principal of the school.

G.R. Barrell, writing about pre-school supervision in the United Kingdom, argues that opening the playground early is a convenience and a privilege, and not an act that adds to the responsibility of the schools.[53] Any supervision would, in Barrell's view, be an act of grace and it would be unfair for parents to add unilaterally to a teacher's duties by delivering a child to school before the appointed time.

Mays v. Essex County Council[54] is a British case that supports Barrell's position. Royston Mays arrived at school before the appointed time and, while playing, split his head open on the asphalt. Although school did not begin until 9:00 a.m., the playground was open at 8:00 a.m. and the students usually congregated at 8:30 a.m. The principal had sent a note to all parents warning them against sending their children to school too early. A directive from the county council instructing teachers to supervise students for 15 minutes both before and after school was not delivered until after the accident. The court concluded that neither the school nor the supervising teacher, who was in the staff room at the other side of the school at the time of the accident, was liable for the accident.

It is advisable that school administrators establish clear hours of supervision both before and after school, and communicate these to the parents. If a child consistently appears at school early, the matter should be raised with the parents. While schools should not be expected to be pre-school babysitters, school administrators should be clear about when supervision will and will not be offered, and there must be some flexibility. When in doubt, however, the teacher should supervise and raise the matter with the principal once the children are safe.

After School Ends

Similar problems of responsibility for supervision arise at the end of the day. What responsibility, if any, does a school official have once a child leaves the school? In most cases, it is reasonable to assume

---

[53] G.R. Barrell, *Teachers and the Law* (London: Methuen, 1978), 303-6.

[54] *Mays v. Essex County Council* (October 11, 1975), *The Times* (London), cited ibid., at 406.

that children will be able to make it home safely from school, although this may not be true if the children are quite young. The foreseeability of harm may be increased if the teacher ignores the parent's express instructions about the child's departure.

In recent years, the issue of the transfer of custody from the school to the parent has become more complex. Where buses are involved, as discussed below, it is a school board responsibility. In the city, where students often walk home from school, there may be a greater responsibility on the teacher. A working parent may require that her child go to a daycare centre on certain days and to her own home on others. Such instructions may be difficult for a young child to follow, and the teacher may be expected to give some guidance. Nonetheless, the ultimate responsibility lies with the parent to ensure that a reasonable system is in place. A teacher will not always be expected to phone to make sure that a parent is there before sending a child home for lunch, but if the child specifically expresses doubt there may be a duty to inquire. Similarly, a teacher should not be expected to babysit students for long periods after school; however, emergencies, such as snowstorms, can extend the time during which school authorities are responsible for students.

In *Barnes v. Hampshire County Council*,[55] 5-year-old children who were always met by parents at an appointed time were released early. A child whose parent had not arrived yet wandered onto a nearby highway and was struck by a car. It was held that early release created a risk that some children might not be met by parents and would try to make their own way home. It was foreseeable that a child might be injured trying to do so, and therefore the school authorities were negligent. Since a parent would probably have met the child if he had not been released early, the release was the cause of the accident and the school was liable. The fact that the release was only five minutes early did not matter, because exact timing was crucial to the particular system upon which parents and school authorities had agreed.

There was, however, no finding of negligence against the teachers or the school in *Bourgeault v. Board of Education St. Paul's Roman Catholic School District No. 20*,[56] because the 14-year-old student, who had fallen from a ladder, had been expressly instructed

---

[55] *Barnes v. Hampshire County Council*, [1969] 3 All ER 746 (HL).

[56] *Bourgeault v. Board of Education St Paul's Roman Catholic School District No. 20* (1977), 82 DLR (3d) 701 (Sask. QB).

to go home. The accident occurred after school hours while the students were decorating the gym for Christmas. A different legal result is likely for students who are permitted or instructed to stay after school. Reliance was placed on an earlier case in which a boy dallied in the playground after school and was injured. In that case the court was clear that the duty of a student after school hours is to go home, and the school was found to have no liability.[57] The age of the student was also a factor in *Bourgeault*; the court accepted that there would be a higher standard of supervision for the young.

An opportunity to clarify a school authority's duty of care to children walking home from school arose in *Dao v. Sabatino and Board of School Trustees (Vancouver)*.[58] The 6-year-old plaintiff was struck by a car while being walked home from school by his 10-year-old sister. The court found that the school authority had met a reasonable standard of care by instructing and drilling students in road safety and by repeatedly warning them against crossing the road at uncontrolled intersections. Unfortunately, since it ruled that no breach of duty occurred, the court found it unnecessary to decide the vexing threshold issue of whether a duty of care even exists under these circumstances.

A recent case from Ontario suggests continuing reluctance to extend the board's duty of care beyond school hours, at least in the case of students who habitually walk home from school. In *Mainville v. Ottawa Board of Education*,[59] the small claims court judge found no negligence when a student who was waiting for his sister in the schoolyard after classes, was injured during a snowball fight. The court noted that the school's policy was to require students to leave the grounds immediately after school. Teacher supervision was limited to patrolling the halls of the school and looking after the children waiting for school buses. In ruling that there was no duty of supervision owed the students once dismissed, the court pointed out that the parents of students who walk to and from school assume that the students are responsible enough to look out for themselves. This decision has been criticized for, among other things, failing to consider that

---

[57] *Edmonson v. Board of Trustees for Moose Jaw School District No. 1* (1920), 55 DLR 563 (Sask. CA).

[58] *Dao v. Sabatino and Board of School Trustees (Vancouver)* (1993), 16 CCLT (2d) 235 (BC SC).

[59] *Mainville v. Ottawa Board of Education* (1990), 75 OR (2d) 315 (Prov. Ct.—Civ. Div.).

the accident apparently occurred during the period when a provincial regulation required the school grounds to be open for the use of pupils.[60]

Dangerous Objects

Common sense dictates that a greater degree of supervision is necessary when a student is handling an inherently dangerous object. Similarly, greater care must be taken to ensure that students do not have unsupervised access to dangerous objects. This was the basis for the schoolmaster's liability when a student was injured by the combustion of phosphorus in *Williams v. Eady*.[61]

Judges have attempted to draw a line between objects that are potentially dangerous and those that are inherently dangerous. Almost anything could fit in the first category, and children must be given some latitude in respect to potentially dangerous objects. This was the view of the court in *Mays v. Essex County Council*:

> There is nothing with which a child cannot hurt himself. There is no game which may not develop into unruly and disorderly conduct. ... Life is full of physical dangers which children must learn to recognize and develop the ability to avoid.[62]

In dealing with a field hockey mishap, Robertson J expressed the same idea more poetically in *Gard v. Board of School Trustees of Duncan*, where he stated:

> No game was ever yet worth a rap
> For a rational man to play,
> Into which no accident, no mishap,
> Could possibly find a way.[63]

A higher degree of supervision is warranted when students are using objects that are inherently dangerous. The problem is deciding which objects fit this label. Things such as a "naked sword, hatchet, loaded gun or an explosive"[64] have been called inherently dangerous, while a "piece of wire, knitting-needle, nail, pen

---

[60] See G. Dickinson, "Lost in Time and Space: Attempting to Draw the Lines Around School Board Duty of Care" (1992-93), 4 *Education and Law Journal* 100.

[61] Supra note 6.

[62] Supra note 54, at 305.

[63] *Gard v. Board of School Trustees of Duncan*, [1946] 2 DLR 441, at 457 (BC CA).

[64] See *Wray v. Essex County Council*, [1936] 3 All ER 97 (CA).

or a scoring knife"[65] have been described as only potentially dangerous. In *Magnusson v. Board of the Nipawin School Unit No. 61*,[66] a piece of broken glass on the fairground adjacent to the school was found to be potentially but not inherently dangerous, and accordingly there was no negligence in failing to supervise that area.

Dangerous Activities

Vocational Classes and Laboratories

When dealing with accidents in cooking, sewing, woodworking, metalworking, or auto repair classes, courts appear to apply the same considerations as when dangerous objects are involved. Thus, where a classroom had gas stoves with open flames the school authorities were negligent in not supplying a guard to prevent the students from being burned, since such an occurrence could have been reasonably anticipated.[67] By analogy, a school would be expected to provide proper protection and to give adequate warnings in the use of microwave ovens in a home economics class.

While sewing is perhaps not usually considered dangerous, a sewing teacher was found liable for not warning a student about one of the few risks associated with the activity. In *Brown v. Essex County Roman Catholic Separate School Board*,[68] a student in a grade 8 family studies class suffered an eye injury when his sewing machine began "sewing on the spot," causing the needle to shatter. Part of the needle embedded itself in the student's eye. The court held that it was reasonably foreseeable that a needle would break if it were permitted to continually sew on the spot, and that the needle would shatter into pieces and strike the machine's user in the eye. That such occurrences are unusual and unlikely did not justify the teacher's failure to guard against them. The teacher failed to discharge her duty of care when she failed to warn the first-year sewer of the particular risks involved in continuing to sew on the spot. Her general warning to stop the machine if a problem arose was insufficient.

---

[65] See *Durham v. Public School Board of North Oxford* (1960), 23 DLR (2d) 711 (Ont. CA).

[66] *Magnusson v. Board of the Nipawin School Unit No. 61* (1975), 60 DLR (3d) 572 (Sask. CA).

[67] *Fryer v. Salford Corporation*, [1937] All ER 617 (CA).

[68] *Brown v. Essex County Roman Catholic Separate School Board*, supra note 44.

The BC Supreme Court took a more lenient approach toward the supervision of shop activities in *Hackl v. Board of School Trustees*,[69] where a student lost an eye when a brass cannon he was crafting flew off a metal lathe and struck him. In the course of its judgment, the court noted that great care must be exercised in supervising the use of hazardous machines by novices. However, the teacher had exercised reasonable care in this case by warning the student to lock the stock properly in place before turning on the lathe. Contrary to the view expressed in *Brown* by the Ontario Supreme Court, the court in *Hackl* stated that it was unreasonable to expect a teacher to explain the precise nature of every potential mishap involved in an activity.

It is clear, however, that the courts will expect teachers supervising hazardous activities to provide at least general instructions regarding the dangers involved and the safety precautions to be followed during such activities.[70] Despite the ruling in *Hackl*, it is probably a safe rule of thumb to require shop teachers and others supervising dangerous activities to describe in some detail the risks involved and how to avoid them. Indeed, in *Scott v. Dunphy*,[71] a teacher was found 35 percent responsible when a student cut his hand on a jointer. Although the teacher had satisfactorily reviewed with his class general safety precautions regarding the use of the machine, he had failed to tell students to check the condition of the push sticks they used to advance boards through the jointer. The push stick used by the plaintiff was worn and it slipped off the board, causing the plaintiff's hand to contact the jointer's blade.

It does not matter how elaborate and specific the prior instructions and warnings given the class by the teacher were if the plaintiff was incapable of benefiting from them. For example, in *Hoar v. Nanaimo Board of School Trustees*,[72] even though a woodworking instructor had handed out 15 pages of safety instructions and conducted a demonstration lesson prior to the students' use of a jointer, he was nevertheless found negligent and 50 percent responsible for failing to repeat the lesson for the benefit of the plaintiff who had been absent for the demonstration. Though

---

[69] *Hackl v. Board of School Trustees*, [1990] BCJ no. 2629 (CA).

[70] *Dunbar v. School District No. 71*, [1989] BCJ no. 728 (BC CA).

[71] *Scott v. Dunphy* (1989), 98 NBR (2d) 339 (QB).

[72] *Hoar v. Nanaimo Board of School Trustees*, [1984] 6 WWR 143 (BC CA).

inconvenient, it appears it is the teacher's duty to repeat missed lessons on a student's return, at least where safety is concerned.

Teachers must also consider the capabilities and special attributes of their students in determining the correct amount of prior instructions and supervision. In recent years, the trend toward academic destreaming and integration of mentally and physically challenged children into regular classes has resulted in classrooms of pupils with a wide array of physical and mental abilities. Thus, the instruction and supervision appropriate for a class of high academic achievers may be insufficent for a class of widely mixed abilities. Where physically or mentally challenged students are involved, even stricter care is required. In *Dziwenka v. Regina*,[73] the Supreme Court of Canada held that a stricter standard of care applied in the supervision of hearing-impaired students using table saws. The Supreme Court upheld the decision of the trial judge who, in finding the teacher negligent, stated that the reason a higher duty of care is owed such students is "because one cannot warn them rapidly of what may be going wrong."[74] It is clear from Dziwenka that teachers must tailor their supervision to the special attributes and needs of all their students.

The necessity for careful and coherent prior instructions should also be an important concern for science teachers supervising students' laboratory activities. When dealing with an experiment that may pose a potential danger to students, a teacher should ensure that appropriate safety precautions are explained and safety equipment provided. In *James v. River East School Division No. 9*,[75] a student was injured when chemicals splattered in her face. She was not wearing safety glasses, and the procedure for the chemistry experiment required her to look into the vessel to determine the progress of the chemical reaction. The teacher was held liable for failing adequately to instruct the students with respect to the potential hazards and, in particular, the possibility of splattering. The court also held that the procedure itself was negligent because it required the student to look into the vessel. It is important to note that the fact that the procedure

---

[73] *Dziwenka v. Regina* (April 10, 1969) (unreported) (Alta. SC—Trial Div.), rev'd. (1970), 16 DLR (3d) 190 (Alta. SC—App. Div.), rev'd. [1972] SCR 419.

[74] Ibid., 16 DLR (3d) 190, at 194.

[75] *James v. River East School Division No. 9*, supra note 34.

was followed in the past without incident did not afford an excuse. In some cases, past practice is used as a defence against a claim of negligence, but if the practice itself is found to be negligent then it provides no defence. A practice does not cease to be negligent just because it is frequently repeated.[76] In addition, it is the general practice that is relevant, not just the practice at one school.

The special risks inherent in the science laboratory have been recognized by school boards, and most have responded by establishing safety programs and guidelines for laboratory conduct.

Sports and Physical Education

Accidents can occur even when no one has been negligent, and a school cannot be an insurer of the safety of all students under its care. It is clear that the courts have no such expectation.[77] There is an inherent risk of injury in most athletic activities, and only if the student is exposed to unreasonable risks will the teacher be considered negligent.[78] Because of the strenuous activities carried on in the gymnasium, the injuries that result from accidents are often very serious and the chance of getting a substantial damages award in the courts is greater. This may explain the relatively large number of physical education-related cases brought before the courts. Because there is some uncertainty about whether trained physical education teachers should exercise a standard of care higher than that of a classroom teacher, we will deal with them separately from regular classroom teachers who engage in athletic instruction as one of many tasks.

Regular Classroom Teachers

As in all other areas of supervision, classroom teachers are required to act as a careful parent would when supervising children

[76] J.C. Anderson, "School Board Negligence—An Update," in J. Balderson and J. Kolmes, eds., *Legal Issues in Canadian Education: Proceedings of the 1982 Canadian School Executive Conference* (Edmonton: Canadian School Executive, 1983), 119, and A.M. Linden, *Canadian Tort Law*, 6th ed. (Toronto: Butterworths, 1997), 187-93.

[77] *Gard v. Board of School Trustees of Duncan*, supra note 63.

[78] See H. Appenzeller, *Physical Education and the Law* (Charlottesville, VA: Michie Co., 1978), for a good summary of the basic principles relevant to negligence and physical education, as well as examples of the outlandish cases for which the United States is known, and J. Barnes, *Sports and the Law in Canada* (Toronto: Butterworths, 1983), for the first comprehensive Canadian book on the topic.

engaged in sports activities. Thus, the question enunciated in *Hall v. Thompson*[79] is, Would a careful parent allow his child to participate under these circumstances? *Hall v. Thompson* held that a careful father would let his 9-year-old son engage in a wrestling match, which is not an inherently dangerous activity. In *Gard v. Board of School Trustees of Duncan*,[80] a boy was struck and injured by another, contrary to the rules, in an unsupervised field hockey game, The teacher who should have been supervising was found not liable. The court decided that a careful parent would have allowed the boy to participate, and, even if there had been supervision, the teacher could not have stopped the game in time to prevent the injury. However, a strong dissenting opinion in *Gard* held that the teacher was negligent—everyone involved in the incident anticipated that the game would be supervised as soon as the teacher escaped her staff meeting. The dissenting judge also felt that it was significant that the boy who caused the injury had had little or no instruction and was thus likely to break the rules.

The lack of prior instruction was clearly an issue in *Petersen v. Board of School Trustees of Surrey*,[81] where a student was injured when he was struck in the eye by a bat that had slipped out of the hands of a batter during a game of rag ball. Despite the relatively low-risk nature of the activity, the court imposed liability because of the teacher-supervisor's failure to warn players of the risk of being hit by a bat and the consequent necessity of paying attention to the batter. The teacher also was found negligent for placing waiting batters in a position where they could be struck by a bat.

A different ruling was reached in *Plumb v. Board of School Trustees of School District No. 65 (Cowichan)*,[82] another case involving an accident in the course of a game with little potential for injury. In *Plumb*, a student was injured while watching a game of catch among three of his mates. Part of the game involved increasing the acceleration of the ball with each throw. When one of the boys missed a catch, the ball struck the plaintiff in the face, injuring his eye. The BC Court of Appeal held that catch was not an inherently dangerous activity; the risk of injury was too small for the school

---

[79] *Hall v. Thompson*, [1952] OWN 133 (HC).

[80] Supra note 63.

[81] *Petersen v. Board of School Trustees of Surrey* (1991), 89 DLR (4th) 517 (BC SC), aff'd. (1993), 104 DLR (4th) 334 (BC CA).

[82] *Plumb v. Board of School Trustees of School District No. 65 (Cowichan)*, [1993] 83 BCLR (2d) 161 (CA).

authorities to be expected to have foreseen it. A prudent parent would not hesitate to permit someone like the plaintiff, a grade 9 student, from participating in the game. Reminiscent of the judicial opinion expressed in *Gard*, the court rejected the imposition of a "'paternalism in respect of boys of teen age ... which would virtually deprive them of that exercise of intelligence demanded of young people of that age in other walks of life.'"[83] Also noteworthy in *Plumb* was the court's application of the tort doctrine applying to spectators of games. As a spectator, the plaintiff was deemed to have accepted the risks ordinarily associated with acts done in the course of, or for the purpose of, the game, except for reckless acts and acts intended to injure someone.

The different rulings in *Petersen* and *Plumb* are most likely attributable to the nature of their respective activities and the degree and nature of their supervision. In *Petersen*, the rag ball game was directly supervised by a teacher who had told students where to stand while waiting for their turn to bat. In *Plumb*, the injury occurred during an informal game begun by students themselves and supervised only to the extent that the entire playground was under general supervision.

Physical Education Teachers

Traditionally, the applicable test in determining whether a physical education teacher was negligent has been that of the careful parent. This was the conclusion reached in *McKay v. Board of Govan School Unit No. 29*,[84] where the school was found liable for injuries to a student who was performing on the parallel bars. The student's lack of experience in the relevant manoeuvres was a critical factor in the decision. In the light of the specialized training of physical education instructors and the complexity of athletic activities, the careful-parent standard may no longer be sensible. A careful parent may not be aware of the inherent risks in such sports as gymnastics or diving. The standard of the competent physical education instructor would be a higher but more appropriate standard; unfortunately, it has not been embraced by the Supreme Court, which continues to cling to the careful-parent test.[85]

---

[83] Ibid., at 166, quoting Keiller Mackay J in *Butterworth v. Collegiate Institute Board of Ottawa (City)*, [1940] 3 DLR 466, at 472 (Ont. SC).

[84] Supra note 14.

[85] See B. Carson, "Negligence ... Reasonably Careful Parent or Competent Instructor in Field" (1968-69), 3 *Ottawa Law Review* 359.

In *Thornton v. Board of School Trustees of School District No. 57*,[86] a decision of the Supreme Court of Canada, a 15-year-old student became a quadriplegic as a result of doing a somersault from a springboard. The physical education teacher was found negligent for not realizing that the addition of a box for jumping created a dangerous situation. He also had failed to stop the exercise to determine the cause of a similar accident in which a student broke his wrist. The teacher had been working on school reports rather than closely supervising the several athletic activities that were taking place in the gymnasium. In spite of the high damages award against the school board, the teacher was not dismissed by the board.

In *Thornton*, both the trial judge[87] and the BC Court of Appeal[88] had held that the teacher had a duty to meet the standard of care of a reasonably skilled physical education instructor rather than that of a careful parent. The Supreme Court of Canada was not required to address that issue on appeal; the court concluded that the teacher was negligent by either standard.

At the appeal level, the BC Court of Appeal stated a four-point test that has been cited in most subsequent cases. There will be no negligence on the part of the physical education instructor who permits a student to engage in gymnastics, such as a somersault off a spring board,

> a. if [the exercise] is suitable to his age and condition (mental and physical);
>
> b. if he is progressively trained and coached to do it properly and avoid the danger;
>
> c. if the equipment is adequate and suitably arranged; and
>
> d. if the performance, having regard to its inherently dangerous nature, is properly supervised.[89]

One of the important factors in assessing the appropriateness of a particular physical activity is the nature and experience of the

---

[86] *Thornton v. Board of School Trustees of School District No. 57* (1978), 83 DLR (3d) 480 (SCC).

[87] *Thornton v. Board of School Trustees of School District No. 57* (1975), 57 DLR (3d) 438 (BC SC).

[88] *Thornton v. Board of School Trustees of School District No. 57* (1976), 73 DLR (3d) 35 (BC CA).

[89] Ibid., at 58.

students concerned. In *Eaton v. Lasuta*,[90] a 12-year-old girl was injured in a piggyback race when she stumbled and broke her leg. The evidence was clear that the young girl was tall, gangling, awkward, uncoordinated, and lacking in athletic talents. Nonetheless, the court concluded that the exercise was appropriate and that the careful parent would have encouraged the girl to participate in the race. A somewhat similar case involving an obese and inexperienced 13-year-old boy produced a different result; the school was found liable for negligence.[91] It was held that injury was foreseeable when the boy was required to make a seven-foot vertical jump. The boy himself had expressed concern about the exercise, which had been in use in this school for only three years. Extra care is required of the physical education instructor teaching a class of students who have either physical or mental disabilities.[92]

In *Myers et al. v. Peel County Board of Education et al.*,[93] a 15-year-old boy was severely injured while attempting a dismount from suspended rings. At trial,[94] the judge applied the higher standard of the reasonably competent physical education teacher used by the Court of Appeal in *Thornton*; but the Ontario Court of Appeal[95] and the Supreme Court of Canada reaffirmed the careful-parent standard as the appropriate one.

In applying the careful-parent test, the Supreme Court stated that the standard will vary depending on the number of students, the nature of the activity, the age of the students, their degree of skill and training, the nature and condition of the equipment used, the competency and capacity of the students, and "a host of other matters."[96] By taking all these factors into account in determining the careful-parent standard, the court suggested that a physical education teacher may be held to a higher standard because of his or her more detailed knowledge of the condition and capacity of the students, the nature of the activity, and the equipment used.

---

[90] *Eaton v. Lasuta* (1977), 2 CCLT 38 (BC SC).

[91] *Boise v. Board of Education of St Paul's Roman Catholic Separate School District No. 20* (1979), 97 DLR (3d) 643 (Sask. QB).

[92] See *Eaton v. Lasuta*, supra note 90, where the court concluded that the girl's awkwardness did not constitute any handicap, and implied that a higher standard would apply if she had been handicapped.

[93] Supra note 16.

[94] *Myers et al. v. Peel County Board of Education et al.* (1977), 2 CCLT 269 (Ont. HC).

[95] *Myers et al. v. Peel County Board of Education et al.* (1978), 5 CCLT 271 (Ont. CA).

[96] Supra note 16, at 279.

Myers is a much more balanced case than *Thornton*, as evidenced by the fact that the trial court and the Supreme Court found the teacher liable while the Court of Appeal did not. The appeal ruling was hailed by some as relieving the fear of Canadian physical education instructors that they would be liable whenever an accident happened.[97] Nonetheless, after examining the four *Thornton* criteria discussed above, the Supreme Court concluded that the inadequate matting and lack of supervision did constitute negligence.

However, as a subsequent case involving a trampoline mishap demonstrates, the Supreme Court of Canada decision in *Myers* has not signalled the imposition of a form of absolute liability on physical education teachers for student injuries. In *Dunn v. Ottawa Board of Education*,[98] a 16-year-old grade 10 student was seriously injured when he landed on his neck on the trampoline during a physical education class. Unlike *Myers*, however, where the teacher knew the plaintiff was intending to practise on the rings, the teacher in *Dunn* was unaware of the student's immediate intention to practise manoevres on the trampoline.

Therefore, it could not be said that the teacher in *Dunn* had permitted a dangerous activity because, unlike the teacher in *Myers*, he did not know that the student would be using the trampoline to perform the routine that resulted in his injury. In holding the teacher and thus the school board blameless, the court shifted the fault entirely to the student, an accomplished athlete who

> was entirely on his own, fully cognizant of the rules of safety, of the dangers involved in somersaulting and confident of his ability which far exceeded that of other students and of his supervisors. He was aware of the requirement of advising his teacher of the risky manoevre he intended to try in the hope ... of receiving a high mark. He said he needed no assistance. He gave no warning of his intention to commence his manoevres on the trampoline.[99]

A close examination of the circumstances in *Myers* and *Dunn* reveals more similarities than differences. It appears that the critical difference explaining the contradictory decisions concerns

---

[97] See, for example, J. Barnes, "*Myers*: Annotation" (1978), 5 CCLT 272.

[98] *Dunn v. Ottawa Board of Education*, [1989] OJ no. 624 (Gen. Div.).

[99] Ibid., at 7.

the attributes of the plaintiffs; while Myers was a relatively inexperienced gymnast, Dunn apparently was an accomplished athlete.

The suitability of a student for a certain athletic endeavour was also at issue in *Thomas v. Board of Education of the City of Hamilton*.[100] In this case, the 16-year-old plaintiff became paralyzed after making a head-on tackle in a football game. Among the allegations of negligence against the coaching staff were that they had played the plaintiff while he was fatigued and out of condition due to a previous injury, that they had not taught proper tackling techniques, and that they should not have allowed the plaintiff to play football because of his "long, lean, swan-neck" physique, which allegedly enhanced his risk of neck injury. The court, however, found as a fact that the plaintiff had recovered from his previous injury, and that he was in condition, fit to play, and not overly fatigued. Moreover, it found that during the entire three years that the the plaintiff had played football, the coaches had taught proper tackling and blocking techniques, including running drills to teach players to keep their heads up and to make contact with their shoulders rather than their heads. As for the plaintiff's "swan-neck" physique, the court found that this theory was not well enough known to reasonably expect the school board and its staff to be aware of it. And, in any event, there was insufficient evidence of a correlation between this neck physique and the type of injury suffered by the plaintiff.

The lack of clarity regarding the precise nature of the standard of care expected of regular classroom teachers (as opposed to physical education specialists) in the supervision of physical education and athletics is representative of the courts' general ambivalence about whether the proper standard of care for teachers should be parentally or professionally based. Almost every case involving the supervision of sports activities by a regular classroom teacher has resulted in the application of the careful-parent test. Even in those cases involving trained physical education instructors, the courts have been reluctant to depart from that test. However, in some cases where the special skill and knowledge of a trained physical education instructor are involved, the courts have advanced the view that the supervisor should be held to the standard of care expected of a reasonable member of that particular subgroup of teachers. This is in keeping with the general tort principle enunciated by Fleming that "[t]hose who undertake work calling for special skill must not

---

[100] *Supra* note 18.

only exercise reasonable care but measure up to the standard of proficiency that can be expected from persons of such profession."[101] In summary, it is unclear when the parentally based (careful parent) as opposed to the professionally based (competent instructor) test will be invoked by the courts in any given case. It would make sense that the more the cause of accident and injury relate to technical aspects of physical education theory and practice, the more one would expect the higher standard of care to be applied.

The Escaping Student

When a teacher fails to supervise students adequately, thereby enabling them to escape school property, he or she may be liable for any harm that befalls these students.[102] This is particularly true with young children. A teacher was held liable when a 4-year-old, left unattended, opened the door and wandered onto a nearby road.[103] In order to avoid the child, a truck driver swerved and died in the resulting accident. The appeal court held that the teacher was liable for the death of the truck driver. Some judges expressed sympathy for the teacher's plight; she had been busy attending to other children at the time of the accident. The fact that this case involved infants in a public nursery made it more difficult for the teacher to meet the standard of care, because of the extreme youth of the children.

The finding of negligence was affirmed by the House of Lords,[104] but the focus of the reasons shifted. Negligence was found not in leaving a child unattended but rather in having a gate that was either unlocked or capable of being opened by a 4-year-old. Equating the teacher's standard to that of the careful parent, the Lords made the following observations:

> I cannot think that it could be considered negligent in a mother to leave a child dressed ready to go out with her for a few moments and then, if she found another of her children hurt and in need of immediate attention, she could be blamed for giving it, without thinking that the child who was waiting to go out with her might wander off into the street.[105]

---

[101] John G. Fleming, *The Law of Torts*, 7th ed. (Toronto: Carswell, 1987), 99.

[102] See Hagenau, supra note 47.

[103] *Lewis v. Carmarthenshire County Council*, [1953] All ER 1403 (CA).

[104] *Carmarthenshire County Council v. Lewis*, [1955] AC 549 (HL).

[105] Ibid., at 561-62.

Later they stated:

> Even a housewife who has young children cannot be in two
> places at once and no one would suggest that she must ne-
> glect her other duties, or that a young child must always be
> kept cooped up.[106]

Thus, even with the escaping child the standard is one of reasonable care, not of constant supervision.

The question of liability for escaping students raises an interesting foreseeability issue in the case of students who routinely
travel to and from school unsupervised. Teachers commonly assume that they will be liable for any injuries befalling students
they negligently allow to escape their supervision. It is difficult
to see, however, how the foreseeability of the risk of accident to a
student who escaped in the middle of the day would be any greater
than the risk to the same student before or after school hours.

What should a teacher do when he or she knows that one of
the students has escaped from the class and possibly from the
school? It may be negligent to pursue the student if that means
leaving the rest of the class unattended. Furthermore, it could be
that chasing the child would cause him or her to panic and run
into the street. On the other hand, a teacher may be confident
that the child can be caught quickly; pursuit may then be reasonable. There is no simple answer, and a reasonable judgment must
be made on the spur of the moment. Often the best course for the
teacher to take is to inform the principal that a student has
escaped; the principal can call the parents or handle the matter
in some other appropriate way. Schools are not intended to be
high-security prisons, nor teachers jailers.[107]

Medical Treatment and Emergencies

First Aid and Health Care

Most provincial school statutes impose a duty on teachers or principals to attend to the health and comfort of their students, and
this duty will apply regardless of what standard the common law
may require. For example, Nova Scotia's Education Act requires
that teachers "attend to the health, comfort, and safety of the

---

[106] Supra note 104, at 566.
[107] See Carson, supra note 85, at 308-9.

students."[108] The court relied on a similar statutory duty in the case of *Board of Education of Toronto and Hunt v. Higgs*,[109] where one teacher was found liable for requiring an injured student to walk with a dislocated hip despite his protests of pain, and another was held negligent for failing to take the student immediately to the nurse despite the student's reluctance to go. The ultimate treatment administered by the nurse was described as "superficial" but there was no claim against her. Not every school has a school nurse, and medical problems are often brought to physical education teachers. They, in particular, and teachers, in general, are well advised to take a first aid course.

The careful-parent rule is also applied in the context of medical treatment. Where a hockey player at a boarding school became seriously ill over a two-week period for no apparent reason, the coach was found negligent for refusing him permission to see a doctor. The court in *Poulton v. Notre Dame College*[110] stated that a "careful father" would have arranged for medical treatment in these circumstances. The fact that this was a boarding school made the teacher's position even more comparable to that of a parent.

Teachers will also be found negligent where they administer improper first aid, such as wrapping a heat stroke victim in a blanket[111] or immersing an infected finger in boiling water.[112] The rationale seems to be that the parental authority to exercise their lay opinion in treating their child's injuries is not delegated to the teacher.[113] It is probably unwise for a teacher to administer first aid to a student except in an emergency, because the improper application of medical treatment can give rise to liability for any harm caused. However, failure to apply first aid in an appropriate situation could also constitute negligence.[114] It is true that most parents do not know first aid, but the large number of

---

[108] Education Act, SNS 1995-96, c. 1, s. 26(1)(n). See also Education Act, RSO 1990, c. E.2, s. 265(j).

[109] Supra note 13. In contrast, the judge in *Ramsden v. Hamilton Board of Education* (1942), 1 DLR 770 (Ont. HC) was impressed by the teacher's speedy application of first aid.

[110] *Poulton v. Notre Dame College* (1975), 60 DLR (3d) 501 (Sask. QB).

[111] *Mogabgab v. Orleans Parish School Board*, 239 So. 2d 456 (La. CA 1970).

[112] *Guerrieri v. Tyson*, 24 A2d 468 (Pa. SC 1942).

[113] Ibid.

[114] See Barrell, supra note 53, at 319-20, for examples of dilemmas that can face the teacher in rendering medical assistance.

children under a teacher's care may raise the standards expected of them in this area.

Medical Consent

With children, as with adults, the administration of medical treatment to a person who has not given a proper consent to the treatment constitutes the intentional tort of either assault or battery, for which damages may be recovered. This consent must be an informed consent—that is, the person consenting must be able to appreciate the nature and the consequences of the particular treatment. When in doubt about whether to seek the consent of the parent or the the child, it is best to acquire the consent of both.

When medical consent is required to treat a child, it is normally the parents or guardians who must give it.[115] Exceptions to this rule occur when the child is sufficiently mature to appreciate the nature and consequences of the treatment and is therefore able to give his or her own consent or where there is an emergency and parental consent cannot be obtained. Whether a child is considered an "emancipated minor" and able to give his own medical consent will depend on a number of factors, including his maturity, whether he is living away from the parental home, and the complexity of the treatment.[116] In most situations a child under 12 years of age will not be considered able to give a medical consent except to simple procedures, such as setting a broken bone. It is not clear that a person *in loco parentis* acquires the parents' power to consent on behalf of the child.[117] Express delegation of such power may be necessary; this underscores the need for detailed permission slips for school outings, which will be discussed below in the section dealing with school board liability and the problems of institutional consent.

Emergencies

Supervising teachers are sometimes confronted with emergency situations requiring an immediate response. A dramatic illustration is provided by *Moddejonge v. Huron County Board of Education*,[118] in

[115] See supra note 123.

[116] See J. Wilson, *Children and the Law* (Toronto: Butterworths, 1978), at 173.

[117] See R. Gosse, "Consent to Medical Treatment: A Minor Digression" (1974), 9 *University of British Columbia Law Review* 56, at 65.

[118] *Moddejonge v. Huron County Board of Education* (1972), 25 DLR (3d) 661 (Ont. HC).

which two young girls tragically drowned. The teacher, who was the coordinator of the outdoor education program, and who held a master's degree in outdoor education, was unable to swim. During an outing, five girls prevailed on the defendant-teacher to drive them to a nearby swimming spot for a brief dip. Aware that there was a dangerous dropoff in the lake, he pointed it out to the girls and warned them to stay away from it. As the teacher paced the beach he became aware of a breeze which was creating some waves, but did not call a halt to the activities.

The breeze carried two of the girls out to the dropoff point where they encountered trouble. One of these girls was a non-swimmer. A third girl came to the rescue and saved one of the imperilled girls but was herself drowned along with the other girl she was attempting to rescue. Because the defendant-teacher could not swim, he had to return to the camp to seek assistance from the other supervising teacher. On these facts, it was not difficult for the court to conclude that the teacher's conduct fell well below that of the careful parent. Liability was imposed for the deaths of the original victim and the rescuer. The supervisor in this case had put himself in the position of being unable to respond to a crisis.

Teachers providing emergency aid, must conduct themselves in a competent manner. As a result of "good Samaritan" laws in some provinces, a rescuer is normally liable only for gross or extreme negligence.[119] However, the definition of "volunteer" likely excludes a supervising teacher as one who is receiving monetary compensation for his or her actions.[120] A teacher, whether acting as a rescuer or not, can incur criminal liability for undertaking acts that endanger life.[121] This underscores the need for teachers who are in charge of field trips or high-risk in-school activities to

---

[119] Volunteer Services Act, RSNS 1989, c. 497. This statute is typical of similar legislation in five other provinces and two territories: see Good Samaritan Act, RSBC 1996, c. 172; Emergency Medical Aid Act, RSS 1978, c. E-8; Volunteer Services Act, RSNS 1989, c. 497; Emergency Medical Aid Act, RSN 1980, c. E-9; Medical Act, RSPEI 1988, c. M-5, s. 50, ordinary negligence standard; Emergency Medical Aid Act, RSNWT 1988, c. E-4; and Emergency Medical Aid Act, RSY 1986, c. 52. For a discussion of the duty to rescue at common law and by statute, see A.M. Linden, *Canadian Tort Law*, 6th ed. (Toronto: Butterworths, 1997), at 284-300.

[120] See, for example, the Nova Scotia Volunteer Services Act, RSNS 1989, c. 497, s. 2.

[121] See Criminal Code, RSC 1985, c. C-46, as amended (herein referred to as "the Code"), ss. 216 and 217.

be trained to cope with emergencies. The elimination of all outings may be a safe legal response, but it is not a good educational
one.

Emergency situations may necessitate medical action either at
the hands of the supervising teacher or on his or her authorization. Problems of medical consent arise most frequently in the
context of field trips and school outings, discussed below. Acquiring parental consent may be impractical, if not impossible. Most
provincial hospital acts or the regulations made under them permit medical treatment without proper consent in order to save
life, limb, or vital organ. There is a legal presumption that a
child consents to life-saving procedures.[122] If the parent objects to
such procedures—for example, a Jehovah's Witness who does not
believe in blood transfusions—special problems arise.[123] Educators might find the following guidelines for doctors, taken from
the British Medical Association's *Handbook of Medical Ethics*,
appendix D, worthy of consideration.

> 1.11 A common problem is that of a patient under the age
> of 16 who requires treatment when no parent or guardian is
> available. Emergencies should not wait for consent and there
> can be little doubt that a court, having regard to parents'
> duty to provide medical care for their child, will uphold the
> doctor's action in providing such care as might reasonably
> anticipate the parents' consent. ...
>
> 1.12 For patients who need treatment for illnesses of lesser
> urgency the doctor must balance the need for treatment
> against the difficulty of contacting the parents.[124]

As far as criminal liability for rendering emergency treatment
is concerned, a teacher could rely on the defence of necessity
under section 8(3) of the Code. The more specific defence for emergency medical aid (stated in section 45 of the Code) applies only
to surgical operations and thus is relevant to doctors rather than
school authorities.

---

[122] See B.M. Dickens, "Non-Treatment in Pediatric Medical Care," paper delivered at the Canadian Association of Law Teachers Conference, Vancouver,
June 1983, at 14-15.

[123] For a comprehensive discussion of a minor's capacity to consent to medical
treatment, see J. Wilson, *Wilson on Children and the Law* (Toronto: Butterworths)
(looseleaf), 5.20-5.26.

[124] Cited in A. Bisset-Johnson, "Medical Consents and Minors," paper delivered at the Consent to Treatment and the Law Conference, Halifax, November
18-19, 1983.

In sum, if a teacher takes reasonable measures to cope with an emergency, a successful lawsuit is unlikely. Remember that the standard expected is not one of perfection but one of reasonableness, in particular that of the careful parent.

Administering Legal Drugs

It has become increasingly common in North American schools for parents to request that school officials administer medication to their children. This medication can be for such maladies as hyperactivity, allergies, diabetes, hemophilia, colitis, or even severe headaches. Although injections or more complicated procedures should only be administered by trained health professionals, such as school nurses, not every school has access to them when needed. The task often falls to teachers, school administrators, or even clerical staff. Teachers of special education classes are particularly vulnerable to this kind of problem.

Obviously drugs should only be administered with parental consent, but that is not usually a problem since it is the parents who request the service. Like the careful parent, a teacher should engage in only such drug administration as he or she is competent to handle. While a school might refuse categorically to undertake the administration of any medicine or medical treatment, the effect of doing so would be to deny some children their right to an education. Whether to establish such a policy is a question for the school board rather than the individual teacher. The teacher should make sure that the school board or the school has insurance coverage for the dispensing of drugs. If no such coverage exists, the safe course is to refuse to administer drugs. A teachers' union probably would support such action.

It seems unfair that parents can insist that teachers administer medication to their children and yet not absolve the teacher from liability. Some US states have responded to this situation by removing the civil liability of those employees who administer drugs in the schools.[125] Of course, there will still be liability for criminal negligence. The best solution for all concerned is to provide training to the teachers so that reasonable competence is assured. Provincial governments and school boards should develop clear policies on drug administration, and boards should ensure that their insurance coverage reflects what is happening

---

[125] See E. White, "Are You Ready To Provide the Health Services Demanded of the Schools" (June 1981), *American School Board Journal*, 25.

in the schools. These policies should be aimed at the safety of the students[126] as well as at the limitation of legal liability.

Emotional Problems

Guidance teachers and instructors of certain types of special education classes must be especially concerned about the mental as well as the physical health of their students. Psychiatric problems are often more difficult to detect than physical problems. This point is illustrated by *Bogust v. Iverson*,[127] in which a young woman committed suicide a few weeks after the guidance counsellor terminated interviews with her. The parents of the student alleged that the teacher was negligent in failing to suggest psychiatric help, failing to inform the parents of their daughter's emotional state, and terminating the interviews.

The US court found no negligence on the part of the teacher, since the suicide of the student was not foreseeable by one who was not trained in psychiatry. The suicide occurred six weeks after the termination of interviews and, in any event, there was no evidence that psychiatric help would have prevented the suicide. Once again the standard applied was that of the careful parent. While teachers of children with emotional problems may be expected to foresee a greater range of risks for their students, they are not expected to become psychiatrists or psychologists.[128]

Criminal Negligence

Teachers and school authorities are subject to the Code provisions on negligence contained in ss. 219 to 221. In addition to their common law duty to take care, school personnel have additional statutory duties that expand the scope of their liability. The conduct required to constitute criminal negligence is more extreme than that needed for a civil action. It must be conduct that shows a "wanton or reckless disregard for the lives or safety

---

[126] See, for example, the Ontario Ministry of Education's *Memorandum 81/84*, which distributes the responsibilities for various medical and paramedical procedures—such as injections, oral medication, and catheterization—among pupils, parents, school board personnel, and health professionals.

[127] *Bogust v. Iverson*, 102 NW 2d 228 (Wisc. SC 1960).

[128] For a more detailed discussion of the liability of school psychologists and counsellors, see L. Fischer and G. Sorenson, *School Law for Counselors, Psychologists, and Social Workers*, 2d ed. (New York: Longman, 1991), chapter 3.

of other persons" as stated in section 219(1) of the Code. Criminal charges will arise only where death or bodily harm results from negligence.

One example of criminal negligence is driving an automobile in such a dangerous fashion as to endanger the lives or safety of others. Another is the case of a parent who wantonly or recklessly disregards foreseeable violence against his or her child at the hands of the other parent.[129] In the light of the special statutory duties imposed on teachers and others to report suspected cases of child abuse and neglect, a teacher might incur criminal liability in an extreme case by failing to discharge his or her reporting duty. Charges of criminal negligence against teachers, however, are very rare in Canada.

---

[129] *R v. Popen* (1981), 60 CCC (2d) 232 (Ont. CA).

3

School Board Liability
for Accidents

The Status of the Board

By this point the perceptive reader will have noticed that the
defendant named in most of the negligence cases is the school
board rather than the individual teacher. In fact, both the teacher
and the school board are sued in most cases; but normally it is
the school board, or more accurately its insurance company, that
pays on behalf of the negligent teacher. The school board is an
independent corporate entity distinct from its individual members. This means that the individual board members will not be
personally liable unless their actions are motivated by malice or
bad faith.[1] Courts are reluctant to reach such a conclusion. If a
school board acts outside its statutory authority or, perhaps, if it
recklessly violates constitutional rights,[2] the members may incur
personal liability.

In Canada, school boards are separate and distinct from municipal councils. Each body is supreme within its own sphere of
authority. In some provinces, vocational schools are directly controlled by cabinet, which in practical terms means the minister of
education operating on the advice of regional advisory boards.
This means that vocational schools must be sued as agents of the
Crown and only in accordance with the special procedural and
time limitations established in the relevant Crown proceedings
statutes.

School boards have a wide range of powers. They can enter
into contracts, hire school personnel, erect and operate school
premises, transport students, supervise students, and perform
other related functions. Provincial education statutes also typically impose mandatory duties on boards. For example, Ontario's

---

[1] *Bowman v. Faber* (1919), 3 WWR 755, at 757 (Sask. KB).

[2] *Wood v. Strickland*, 420 US 308 (1975).

Education Act requires school boards, among other things, to keep the school buildings in proper repair and to make provision for adequately insuring themselves, their employees, and volunteers against claims in respect of accidents to pupils.[3] Boards can be sued for breach of any statutory or common law duties in relation to any of their activities; however, courts are unlikely to award damages solely for breach of a statutory duty. Under some circumstances, a school board, like any other corporation, can also be sued for breach of contract, but that topic is beyond the scope of this book. School boards are also liable for on-the-job injuries to their own employees, but such losses are handled under statutory workers' compensation schemes rather than tort law.[4] We are concerned instead with the tort liability of school boards in their capacities as supervisors of students, occupiers of premises, and transporters of students.[5]

Vicarious Liability

Cases involving the negligence of teachers, principals, or other school employees usually result in a finding of liability against the relevant school board under the doctrine of vicarious liability. If a teacher or other employee of the school board is negligent, then he or she is personally liable in damages; but the employing school board, which is normally in a better position to compensate the victim, is often the primary defendant. In some cases the school board may even be liable for negligence where the employed teacher is excluded from liability by statute.[6]

Definition

J.G. Fleming, one of the leading authorities on tort law, defines vicarious liability as follows:

---

[3] See the Education Act, RSO 1990, c. E.2, s. 170(9).

[4] For example, the Nova Scotia statute is the Workers' Compensation Act, RSNS 1989, c. 508.

[5] See J. Barnes, "Tort Liability of School Boards to Pupils," in L. Klar, ed., *Studies in Canadian Tort Law* (Toronto: Butterworths, 1977), 189ff., where he suggests that school boards are liable either "qua supervisor or qua occupier." We have added transportation as a separate category but it might be considered a subset of supervision.

[6] See *McKay v. Board of Govan School Unit No. 29 Saskatchewan* (1968), 64 WWR 301 (SCC). In addition to Saskatchewan, other provinces, such as Prince Edward Island, do provide some statutory exclusions of teacher liability.

> We speak of vicarious liability when the law holds one person
> responsible for the misconduct of another, although he is him-
> self free from personal blameworthiness or fault.[7]

The doctrine has its origin in the law of master and servant;
originally, under the common law, the employer was liable only
for acts that resulted from the employer's order. Vicarious liability has now been expanded to all torts committed by an employee
while acting in the course of employment and extends well beyond actions that were expressly commanded by the employer. At
present the rationale for the doctrine of vicarious liability is clearly
the promotion of reasonable loss allocation. It is the school board
and not the teacher who can afford to compensate the victim and
who is insured for such losses. School boards have an economic
incentive to prevent accidents and discipline their employees for
unreasonable conduct.

Joint Tortfeasors and Indemnity

Under the doctrine of vicarious liability both the teacher and the
school board are tortfeasors; each is responsible for the full loss.
However, the loss can only be claimed once; as long as the school
board has adequate insurance, it normally pays without dispute.
It should be understood, however, that subrogation rights legally
entitle boards' insurers to make decisions about defending lawsuits, including defending on the grounds that a teacher was
acting outside the scope of his or her employment. Teachers and
other school employees should therefore consider obtaining, if
possible, their own liability insurance for accidents that occur
outside the course of employment. At common law an employee is
not required to indemnify his or her employer for losses, but
statutes in many jurisdictions now allow contribution between
joint tortfeasors.[8] This allows one tortfeasor to recoup some of
the loss from another defendant. In the English case of *Ryan v.
Fildes*,[9] the school authority recovered 100 percent indemnity from
a teacher who rendered a student deaf by a cuff on the ear.

---

[7] J.G. Fleming, *The Law of Torts*, 7th ed. (Sydney: The Law Book Company,
1987), 339.

[8] See H.C. Cosgrove, "The Teacher and the Common Law," in A. Knott, K.
Tronc, and J. Middleton, eds., *Australian Schools and the Law*, 2d ed. (St Lucia:
University of Queensland Press, 1980), 71.

[9] *Ryan v. Fildes*, [1938] 3 All ER 517 (KB).

If a Canadian school board is sued in vicarious liability, the board probably will be entitled to indemnity from the teacher's insurance policy, if any, to the extent of the policy coverage. The House of Lords in *Lister v. Romford Ice Co.*[10] held that employers were entitled to be indemnified against their employees who were guilty not only of intentional or wanton misconduct, but also of mere negligence. This principle has been adopted by the Ontario Court of Appeal.[11] Even if the teacher was not joined as a party by the plaintiff, the school board is probably entitled to seek indemnity against the teacher in third-party proceedings; as a matter of practice, however, indemnity is rarely sought in Canadian school cases.

Course of Employment

The concept of "course of employment" is an elusive one. In recent times most actions of employees have been held to be in the course of employment, even those that have been expressly forbidden by the employer.[12] It appears that even a breach of an order must be such as to put the employee outside the scope of his job to eliminate vicarious liability. If the employee is on a frolic of his own and, in effect, acting as a stranger in respect to his or her employer, then no liability attaches to the employer.[13] Actions that are a means of carrying out the job—albeit negligently or even in breach of express rules—are still in the "course of employment." In *Moddejonge v. Huron County Board of Education*,[14] the outrageous actions of the outdoor education teacher in exposing his students to the risk of drowning were found to be within the scope of his employment. A good formulation of the relevant test is whether a wrongful act is "a mode of performing the general duties of the servant's employment: whether the servant was about his master's business at the time."[15]

---

[10] *Lister v. Romford Ice Co.*, [1957] AC 555 (HL).

[11] *Fenn v. City of Peterborough* (1979), 104 DLR (3d) 174, at 219-21 (Ont. CA). Fleming, supra note 7, at 238-39, suggests that the policy considerations against indemnity are strong.

[12] *Holohan v. Dunfield* (1982), 133 DLR (3d) 267 (NB QB). This principle was established earlier in *CPR v. Lochardt*, [1942] AC 591 (PC).

[13] See Fleming, supra note 7, at 352-54.

[14] *Moddejonge v. Huron County Board of Education* (1972), 25 DLR (3d) 661 (Ont. HC).

[15] Supra note 8, at 70.

One notable case in which the action of a teacher was held to be outside the scope of her employment is *Beauparlant v. Board of Trustees of Separate School Section No. 1 of Appleby*.[16] Teachers decided to transport approximately 70 students to a nearby town for a concert that was being held in honour of a priest's birthday. Transportation for the outing was a stake-body truck provided by a citizen in the community. The truck had not been inspected for safety. While it was proceeding to its destination, with the students riding in the back, either the stakes or the chain around the sides of the truck broke, and several children were thrown onto the highway and seriously injured. The court concluded that the activity was unconnected to the course of studies. No board permission had been obtained for the trip, and the school board was found not liable for the accident because the teachers were acting outside the scope of their authority.

A spontaneous class outing to a local restaurant in a teacher's car could expose the teacher to personal liability. It is advisable to seek a general approval for such trips either from the principal or, preferably, the school board itself. Activities related to the course of studies are much more likely to be found to be within the course of employment. The school board was held vicariously liable in a case where a 14-year-old student was instructed to poke the fire in the teachers' room, and was injured when her pinafore caught fire.[17] The ruling was made in spite of the fact that the fire was being prepared so the teacher could have a hot lunch. The courts have taken a broad approach to defining the scope of employment, and school boards will usually be found liable for the acts of their employees.

In earlier cases, arguments were made that a school board would not incur vicarious liability for actions taken by teachers acting as delegates of the parent rather than as agents of the state. This argument was advanced with respect to both the supervision of students and the administration of discipline. On the matter of supervision, the argument of delegated parental authority was clearly rejected in the Australian case of *Ramsay v. Larsen*.[18] The duty to supervise was a state responsibility incumbent on both the school board and the teacher as agents of the state.

---

[16] *Beauparlant v. Board of Trustees of Separate School Section No. 1 of Appleby*, [1955] 4 DLR 558 (Ont. HC).

[17] See *Smith v. Martin and the Corporation of Kingston*, [1911] 2 KB 775 (CA).

[18] *Ramsay v. Larsen* (1964), ALR 1121 (Aust. HC).

Intentional Wrongs

Vicarious liability arises not just from an employee's negligence but also from his or her intentional wrongdoing. In the latter case, the liability of the employer is more narrowly defined on the basis of "real or ostensible authority" rather than by the broader test of "course of employment."[19] This is the case as long as the intentional wrong was in furtherance of the employee's duties and resulted from either excessive zeal or bad judgment.[20] The question is whether the wrong is personal or work-related. A school board could be held vicariously liable for a battery that resulted from the too-forceful disciplining of a student, so long as the conduct was not extreme. Of course, the existence of either a school or a school board rule against corporal punishment is strong evidence that the teacher has exceeded his or her authority, and the board as employer will probably escape liability.

Employers have been found both vicariously liable and not liable for sexual assaults committed by their employees against the children in their charge. Two recent cases from British Columbia help illustrate how courts distinguish among such cases. In *J.-T.(G.) v. Griffiths*,[21] the infant plaintiffs sued the program director of the Boys and Girls Club for damages for sexual assaults he had committed against them. Even though the assaults had occurred at the defendant's home outside his hours of work, the trial judge found the defendant-club vicariously liable. On appeal, the BC Court of Appeal overturned the finding of vicarious liability, ruling that merely providing an employee an opportunity to gain a victim's trust and then to assault him or her was insufficient to impose vicarious liability on an employer. There must be evidence that the wrongdoing amounted to an abuse of the very authority conferred on the employee by the employer for the purpose of doing his job. There must be some likelihood that the powers conferred on the employee would increase the probability of a wrong occurring.

In this case, no special powers or authority had been given to the program director. The boys and girls in the club were not under the club's authority nor did the club or its employees stand *in loco parentis* toward them. Under these circumstances, the risk of a wrong occurring was deemed to be no greater than when

---

[19] See Fleming, supra note 7, at 354.

[20] Ibid., at 354-57.

[21] *J.-T.(G.) v. Griffiths*, [1997] BCJ no. 695 (CA).

any adult comes into contact with children for social activities. The court therefore held that no vicarious liability should be imposed on the employer. There is an obvious distinction to be drawn between the role of the director in this case and that of a teacher. Teachers enjoy both statutory and common law authority over pupils, the latter deriving from the centuries-old doctrine of *in loco parentis*. Moreover, the relationship between teachers and pupils has been viewed in law as one of the strongest forms of fiduciary trust.[22]

On this reasoning, there appears to be little reason why a board that employs a teacher who commits the intentional tort of sexual assault on a pupil should not be held vicariously liable, absent some unusual circumstances distancing the teacher's misconduct from the teacher–pupil relationship created under his or her employment. However, to date, courts have been reluctant to impose such liability.[23]

There can be a fine line, however, between acts deemed personal to the employee and those deemed to be in the furtherance of his or her authorized employment duties. For example, in *B.(P.A.) v. The Children's Foundation*,[24] the same court that dismissed the plaintiff's claim for vicarious liability in *J.-T.(G.) v. Griffiths* imposed vicarious liability on a charitable foundation that employed a residential counsellor who sexually abused a child residing in one of its group homes. The court held that the employee's conduct involved breach of a fiduciary relationship since he had been acting *in loco parentis* in the residential setting. Unlike *J.-T.(G.)*, this was not a case of the employer merely providing an opportunity for assault to occur, but rather one where the employer increased the probability of such an occurrence by conferring a powerful surrogate parent status on the employee. When an employer accepts parental authority over a child, it is deemed also to accept responsibility for the consequences of the abuse of that authority by an employee to whom such authority

---

[22] See G.V. La Forest, "Off-Duty Conduct and the Fiduciary Obligations of Teachers" (1997), 8 *Education & Law Journal* 119.

[23] R. Fossey and T. DeMitchell, "'Let the Master Answer': Holding Schools Vicariously Liable When Employees Sexually Abuse Children" (1996), 25 *Journal of Law & Education* 575. The authors point out that US courts have been inconsistent in imposing vicarious liability for sexual abuse by teachers (at 586). They call for the courts' recent readiness to hold police and health authorities vicariously liable for their employees' sexual misconduct to be extended to cases involving school boards (at 589-99).

[24] *B.(P.A.) v. The Children's Foundation*, [1997] BCJ no. 692 (CA).

is delegated. The court recognized, however, the need to pay attention to the particular context of each case of this nature, especially the nature of the authority conferred on the employee and how likely it was that such authority would enhance the probability of the wrongful act's occurrence.

It is too early to say what influence these two BC cases will have on subsequent court decisions concerning school board vicarious liability for intentional torts, especially sexual assaults, committed by teachers against students. Hitherto, not surprisingly, there has been scant evidence of such conduct being drawn into the ambit of vicarious liability under the agency doctrine of ostensible authority. After all, it is an unpalatable conclusion to impute authority to commit such acts. The BC cases, however, seem to open the door somewhat to school board vicarious liability by virtue of the *power relationship* created between teachers and their victims by the board's mere employment of the former.

One should note that, regardless of whether the school board is vicariously liable in a given case, it is still possible to find its members and individual officials (such as principals and superintendents) personally or primarily liable for negligence. This negligence usually concerns supervisors' failure to notify the board in the case of a teacher whom they knew or ought reasonably to have known was a threat to students, or the board's failure to act on such information if given. Thus in *Lyth v. Dagg*[25] the plaintiff sued his former teacher, the shcool board, and others for damages for battery relating to sexual assaults committed against him by the teacher. The BC Supreme Court determined that there was insufficient evidence to conclude that the superintendent to whom allegations about this teacher had been made before the assaults, either knew or ought reasonably to have known of the teacher's propensity to commit such an offence. However, it is clear that where the evidence does lend itself to such a conlusion, principals, superintendents, and other superiors of the offender could be held primarily liable for negligence. Of course, since this negligent conduct would have occurred in the course of their employment, the school board would doubtless be held vicariously liable for it.

It is important to distinguish between civil and criminal liability in the context of vicarious liability. An employer does not incur criminal liability for the actions of his or her employees; in

---

[25] *Lyth v. Dagg* (1988), 46 CCLT 25 (BC SC).

a criminal case—for example, a charge of assault stemming from corporal punishment—the teacher alone is charged personally.

Independent Contractors

An independent contractor is distinguished from an employee by the amount of control the person contracting for the services exercises over the worker. There is no question that teachers and most school personnel are employees, not independent contractors. However, there are some situations, where school boards contract work out to independent contractors; in those cases, the doctrine of vicarious liability does not apply. The distinction between employees and independent contractors must be made on the facts of each case.

This distinction arises most frequently in the context of transporting students, discussed below. Different circumstances were involved, however, in *Ellis v. Board of Trustees for Moose Jaw Public School District and Blondin Roofing Products Limited*.[26] Workmen repairing the school roof set up equipment that included ropes and pulleys. There was no question that the workmen were independent contractors, and they were found negligent when a pupil received severe head injuries from falling wood. Apparently, students had ignored the warnings of both the principal and the workmen and were swinging on the ropes at recess. The court clearly stated that the school board could not delegate its responsibility to supervise to an independent contractor on the premises. Indeed, the presence of the workmen created abnormal risks and the board, through the principal, was negligent in not taking greater care for the safety of the students. The contractors and the board were jointly liable, and no issue of vicarious liability arose.

Safe Transportation

Although it is by no means the case that under provincial education statutes school boards are uniformly required to provide transportation for students, it is clear that where they do—whether under statutory obligation or voluntarily—they must ensure a reasonably safe transportation system. Whether they maintain

---

[26] *Ellis v. Board of Trustees for Moose Jaw Public School District and Blondin Roofing Products Limited*, [1946] 2 WWR 19 (Sask. CA).

their own fleet of buses or contract service from a private carrier, boards must carefully and constantly monitor school bus safety.

Independent Contractors and Employees

Where school boards purchase their own buses and hire the drivers, an employment relationship giving rise to vicarious liability on the part of the board is clearly established. Vicarious liability for independent bus services, however, will depend on the degree of board control over the drivers. In *Baldwin v. Lyons and Erin District High School Board*,[27] the Ontario Court of Appeal held that the school board did not exercise sufficient control to change the contractual relationship to one of master and servant. In that case, the agreement between the board and the bus company specified the routes and times involved. In *Mattinson v. Wonnacott*,[28] a 5-year-old child, who was to be let off the bus at his lane, got off the bus while it was waiting at another school, without the driver's noticing, and was hit by a car. In that case, the board exercised considerable control over the bus contractor, and had given him a copy of the board's transportation policy. On these facts the court concluded that the bus company was a servant of the board and not just an independent contractor. The school board was held to be vicariously liable.

Standard of Care

The court in *Mattinson v. Wonnacott* would have found the board liable for negligence even apart from the issue of vicarious liability. By accepting responsibility for arranging transportation, the board had extended its duty of supervision to the busing operation. The board failed to instruct the bus company with respect to loading and unloading procedures and ignored suggestions from the bus company that a teacher was needed to supervise the process. In the opinion of the court, this conduct was in breach of the standard of the careful parent.

A board is expected to adhere to the standard of reasonableness but is not expected to ensure the safe transportation of students. In *Hoyt v. Hay and Board of School Trustees for District*

---

[27] *Baldwin v. Lyons and Erin District High School Board* (1961), 36 DLR (2d) 290 (Ont. CA), aff'd. (1962), 36 DLR (2d) 244 (SCC).

[28] *Mattinson v. Wonnacott* (1975), 8 OR (2d) 654 (HC).

20,[29] a grade 1 student was injured when he was struck by a car after alighting from a commercial bus. He could have taken a regular school bus home one hour later, which would have dropped him off on his own side of the road. The school gave parents the choice of having the students wait an extra hour until the older students were released, or taking the commercial bus that left one hour earlier. The parents opted for the commercial bus even though their son would have to cross the road. No liability was placed on the school board because it had no control over the commercial bus and because it was not required to provide a bus immediately after school.

Teachers' Vehicles

Teachers often transport students to and from sporting events or other extracurricular activities in their own vehicles. As long as the teachers are acting in the course of their employment, then the school board will be vicariously liable and should be insured against such losses. In many schools specific people are designated to transport students to events, and in some cases a school vehicle may be provided. Often physical education teachers are given such a designation and the school pays the necessary increase in insurance premiums. If there is a school rule against teacher transportation of students, a board may still be vicariously liable when such conduct occurs because of the broad definition of "course of employment."

If the teacher does transport students, and there is either no board policy or an express prohibition, then he or she should make sure that his or her individual insurance policy covers the situation. According to section 91 of Nova Scotia's Insurance Act,[30] a regular automobile insurance policy will not cover a person who is "carrying passengers for compensation or hire." Section 91(4) lists certain categories that do not fall within this exception; paragraph (v) was added in 1982 to cover "the occasional and infrequent use by the insured of his automobile for the transportation of children to or from school or school activities conducted within the educational program."[31] This means that a teacher's regular

---

[29] *Hoyt v. Hay and Board of School Trustees for District 20* (1978), 23 NBR (2d) 497 (QB).

[30] RSNS 1989, c. 231, as amended.

[31] Similar provisions may be found in other provincial Insurance Acts. See, for example, Insurance Act, RSO 1990, c. I.8, s. 250(4)(e) and Insurance Act, RSA 1980, c. I-5, s. 311(4)(d).

insurance policy will apply to some but not all cases of student transportation. Transportation must be in the insured's own vehicle, must be infrequent, and must concern activities within the educational program. Neither a spontaneous lunch outing to a local restaurant nor the situation in *Beauparlant*[32] would be covered by paragraph (v). If there is any payment by the students for the transportation, either in cash or in kind, the chances of the insurance coverage applying diminish. Any teacher in doubt about his or her insurance coverage should consult an insurance agent and possibly a lawyer before transporting students. Acquiring proper insurance coverage is preferable to curtailing the services entirely.

Supervision by Students

Sometimes senior students may be given responsibility for the safe transportation of younger students. One example is *Jacques v. Oxfordshire County Council*,[33] in which two 14-year-old student prefects were designated to supervise the other students on the bus. In spite of the fact that one of the supervised students suffered an eye injury from an object thrown by another student, the student prefects were found to have conducted themselves as reasonable parents would have done. If there had been a finding of negligence the school board would have been liable for the inadequate supervision. The position of student traffic patrols is less clear,[34] but the same reasoning should apply. In most cities, school boards are not required to provide safety patrols or crossing guards, but if they do they are liable for the actions of the guards.

Reasonable Supervision

School boards are liable by virtue of vicarious liability for the failure of teachers and other school personnel to properly supervise students. Thus, the many cases on teacher liability considered in chapter 2 are also relevant here. There are, however, some additional duties imposed on boards and principals, as their agents, to devise a safe supervision system. Furthermore, there

---

[32] Supra note 16.

[33] *Jacques v. Oxfordshire County Council* (1968), 66 LGR 440 (Ox. Assiz.), reproduced in G.R. Barrell, *Legal Cases for Teachers* (London: Methuen, 1970), 330.

[34] See *Eyres v. Gillis and Warren Ltd.* (1940), 4 DLR 747 (Man. CA).

are provisions in statutes, regulations, and board policies that apply uniquely to boards. Boards are also responsible for the actions of non-teaching employees such as janitors.

Adequate Supervision Systems

It is the school board through its frontline agent, the school principal, that is responsible for establishing and maintaining a safe supervision system for students. The distinction between the liability of teachers and the liability of principals with regard to supervision is exemplified in *Dyer v. Board of School Commissioners of Halifax*.[35] A wide range of factors must be considered in devising an adequate supervision system—for example, the existence of an allurement or distraction for children on the school grounds,[36] the ratio of supervising teachers to pupils, the activity in which the students are engaged, the age and maturity of the students, the weather conditions, the nature of the students, and the geographic layout of the supervised area. These and other factors will be examined in the context of the following cases, which are divided into those concerning the teaching staff and those concerning other employees.

Teaching Staff

As we have seen, school authorities have a duty to provide reasonable supervision, not constant attention. The degree of supervision that will be considered reasonable diminishes as the age of the child increases. When a teenage pupil was injured in a scuffle involving sheath knives, Lord Denning held that there was no negligence in the supervision of the playground.[37] The case involved two prefects who were normally on duty but were away at the time marking trails for a cross-country run. In their absence the master walked through the yard a couple of times. The judge concluded that more supervision would not have prevented the accident, which occurred in a flash.

---

[35] *Dyer v. Board of School Commissioners of Halifax* (1956), 2 DLR (2d) 394 (NS SC), and see, in particular, the discussion of the case in chapter 2 in the text accompanying note 39.

[36] The presence of the roof repairmen on the schoolgrounds in *Ellis*, supra note 26, is an example.

[37] See *Clarke v. Monmouthshire County Council* (1954), 52 LGR 246 (CA).

The same conclusion was reached by the Supreme Court of
Canada in *Board of Education of Toronto and Hunt v. Higgs*.[38]
The plaintiffs in *Higgs* had alleged that the system of supervision
employed by the principal on the day of the incident was inappropriate because there were not enough supervising teachers on
duty. The Supreme Court disagreed, stating that, given the number
and ages of the children at the school, the principal had no reason to believe that the system he had in place—four teachers to
supervise 750 pupils—was anything less than reasonable. The
court also rejected the suggestion that the snowy condition of the
schoolyard constituted an unusual circumstance justifying the
deployment of additional teachers. Critical to the court's judgment was the finding that even had more teachers been deployed,
the incident in question, which was quite spontaneous, would
probably still have occurred.

In *Adams v. Board of School Commissioners for Halifax*,[39] a stone-
throwing incident at recess resulted in an eye injury to an innocent
bystander. At the original jury trial, the teacher was absolved of
liability because she was attending to an incident in another part
of the yard when the stone throwing occurred; the court held that
she could not reasonably be expected to be in two places at once.
The policy followed in this and other city schools was to have one
teacher supervise the girls' yard and another the boys' yard. After
being instructed on the school board regulations, which could be
read as requiring constant supervision, the jury found the board
negligent. On appeal, the matter was sent back for a new trial. The
appeal court held that, in his instructions to the jury, the trial
judge had overstated the effect of the regulations, which were only
board guidelines. It held that the careful-parent standard was the
proper standard to apply, and breach of the regulations was not
negligence *per se*. At most, the regulations indicated the board's
expectations; meeting those expectations was not necessarily reasonable supervision, nor was breaching them necessarily negligence.
If the regulations had been approved by cabinet, or if they had
been in statutory form, their impact would have been greater.

The extra force of statutory statements of the school's duty to
supervise is illustrated by *Schade v. Winnipeg School District
No. 1*.[40] At the trial level, the judge held that the common law

---

[38] *Board of Education of Toronto and Hunt v. Higgs* (1959), 22 DLR (2d) 49 (SCC).

[39] *Adams v. Board of School Commissioners for Halifax*, [1951] 2 DLR 816 (NS CA).

[40] *Schade v. Winnipeg School District No. 1*. (1959), 27 WWR 546 (Man. CA).

duty of the careful parent had been modified by a statute that did not mandate supervision of activities that were not part of the educational program. Thus, there was no liability when a 13-year-old student was injured by tripping over a construction stake during a scrub baseball game held at noon. The Court of Appeal concluded that the child was the author of his own misfortune. Bearing in mind his age, intelligence, and knowledge of the circumstances, he should have taken greater care for his own safety. Emphasis was placed on the need for the child to develop independence and responsibility. Today, higher statutory standards are imposed in most provinces than was the case in *Schade*.

Even in the 1950s the courts imposed higher standards of care when young children were involved. *Brost v. Board of Trustees of Eastern Irrigation School Division No. 44*[41] involved an injury to a 6-year-old child who fell from a swing. The principal and school board were found liable for failure to supervise young children on the swings. While one of the factors considered was a policy handbook that encouraged teachers to supervise play activity, the critical point was that the risk was foreseeable.

Other Employees

Liability of school boards for the acts of their non-teaching employees is less clearly defined than their liability for their teachers' actions. While it is likely that a board will be held to the same general standards for the performance of a student teacher, there may be a lower standard for a teacher's aide. The appropriate standards for a school crossing-guard or a lunch monitor also have not been clearly settled. A bus driver who has the authority to discipline or suspend unruly student passengers will be held to the same standards of reasonable force as a teacher.

A school board is vicariously liable for any of its employees, but there will be a question as to what standard applies in different situations. A janitor who injured a student while the student was helping to move a piano was held to a standard of reasonable care.[42] The court had no doubt that he was acting as an agent of the school board in providing and maintaining furniture, and thus he was protected by the statutory limitation period. There was no

---

[41] *Brost v. Board of Trustees of Eastern Irrigation School Division No. 44*, [1953] 3 DLR 159 (Alta. CA).

[42] See *Moffatt v. Dufferin County Board of Education*, [1973] 1 OR 351 (CA).

suggestion that the janitor had to meet the standard of the careful parent.

The court stated in *Bourgeault v. Board of Education St Paul's Roman Catholic School District No. 20*[43] that a caretaker's duty was not to supervise students but simply to exercise reasonable care for their safety. When a 14-year-old girl returned to the school gym after dismissal, she was injured in a fall from a ladder. The caretaker had earlier warned students not to climb on the ladder, and when they assured him that they would get down, he left. This was considered reasonable conduct. A more extensive duty of supervision applied only to teachers.

Field Trips and Extracurricular Activities

Educational outings are more common than they used to be, and the duty to supervise extends to such extracurricular activities. Wisely, many school boards have detailed regulations and procedures for school excursions. G.R. Barrell offers some sound advice for teachers who may be involved in school outings—he suggests that careful attention be paid to the student–teacher ratio, that teachers familiarize themselves with the relevant regulations, that proper insurance coverage be obtained, and that permissions be sought from both the school board and the parents.[44] Barrell also recommends that supervising teachers be familiar with first aid and that they obtain consent forms from the parents for necessary medical treatment. These preventive measures are the best way to avoid accidents and potential lawsuits.

Increased Risks

Often the risks of injury to students increase when they leave familiar school territory. It is logical that a teacher who takes his or her class on a boat ride should make sure that they are all wearing life jackets. Taking students to a fair normally involves greater risks than taking them to a play or a museum. Accidents can happen even at a museum, however, as illustrated by a US case where one of the students on a class trip to a museum was the victim of a racially motivated assault.[45] The court ruled that

---

[43] *Bourgeault v. Board of Education St Paul's Roman Catholic School District No. 20* (1977), 82 DLR (3d) 701 (Sask. QB).

[44] See Barrell, supra note 33, at 349-62.

[45] W.P. Hagenau, "Penumbras of Care Beyond the Schoolhouse Gate" (1980), 9 *Journal of Law and Education* 201, at 209.

such harm was not foreseeable and imposed no liability. The outcome would likely be different if a student were left to find his or her own way home from a high-crime area. If the student were sexually assaulted, the teacher's negligence might be a contributing cause. It is also possible that students on a school outing might harm the person or property of a third party. In such circumstances the school board might be found liable.[46] As the range of foreseeable risks increases, the school's standard of care rises.

Teachers supervising field trips and other out-of-school excursions should be particularly wary of deviating from scheduled activities, thus bringing into play increased risks of accident and injury. In *Moddejonge v. Huron County Board of Education*,[47] an unscheduled side-trip to a swimming hole transformed a low-risk excursion into one with high risks, with tragic results. Unscheduled, last-minute deviations are, by their nature, unplanned. Supervisors, therefore, are usually left without the information, resources, skills and assistance needed to reduce or manage potentially higher levels of risk. In *Moddejonge*, had swimming been a scheduled activity, it would have been a relatively simple matter to ensure supervision by a trained lifesaver.

The same point is illustrated particularly well in *Bain v. Calgary Board of Education*.[48] In this case, students on a foresty products tour convinced the supervising teacher to allow them to climb a mountain during their free time instead of going to a movie as planned. During the unsupervised climb, the plaintiff slipped and fell down the side of the mountain, striking his head on a rock. He suffered a serious brain injury, resulting in an award of damages of more than $3 million against the supervisor and his school board. In finding the teacher negligent, the court held that, by allowing the activity, the teacher had changed the fundamental nature of the program and created a high duty of care. The teacher's first failure was permitting the climb. Having permitted it, however, he was under an obligation to take reasonable steps to reduce the risks involved in the activity by supervising and controlling it. The teacher did not remain to supervise the climb, nor was he able to give proper warnings or instructions because he was unfamiliar with the terrain and had taken no steps to consult maps or local residents. Reminiscent of *Myers*

---

46 See *Dorset Yacht Co. v. Home Office*, [1970] AC 1004 (HL).

47 *Moddejonge v. Huron County Board of Education*, supra note 14.

48 *Bain v. Calgary Board of Education* (1993), 14 Alta. LR (3d) 319 (QB).

et al. v. Peel County Board of Education et al.,[49] the court stated
that the teacher should have expected reckless behaviour from at
least some of the students.

Mandatory Versus Optional School Outings

When a school outing is mandatory, it becomes part of the school
program and the regular duty to supervise arises. If the outing or
extracurricular activity is optional, there may be no duty to supervise. The fact that the school makes its gymnasium available to
students after school hours does not necessarily give rise to a duty
to supervise. However, such a duty might arise if it is known that
the permitted activity is likely to be dangerous.[50] The requisite
degree of supervision is determined largely by the amount of control that school authorities exercise over the activity.[51] A greater
responsibility for supervision will exist for a club with a faculty
adviser than for one involving students alone; the extent to which
the extracurricular activity is encouraged by the school is important.

It should also be noted that the fact that the activity which
gave rise to an injury was a student-conceived deviation from a
program that school authorities originally approved does not transfer the burden of legal responsibility from the school to the students, especially where, as in *Bain*, the students sought and obtained a supervisor's permission.

Board Authorization

Any teacher leading a student excursion should make sure that
it is authorized by the school board. In some cases the principal
can give such authorization but, if in doubt, it is best to check
with the board itself. Many boards have adopted elaborate forms
that must be completed by either the teacher, the principal, or
both before a school outing can take place. Failure to obtain a
proper board authorization could result in a finding that the
teacher was acting outside the course of his or her employment.
Although such a finding is unlikely, *Beauparlant*[52] illustrates that
the teacher can be found personally liable for any accidents that

---

[49] *Myers et al. v. Peel County Board of Education et al.* (1981), 17 CCLT 269,
at 279 (SCC).

[50] See *Whitlock v. University of Denver*, 712 P2d 1072 (Colo. CA 1985).

[51] See Hagenau, *supra* note 45, at 210 and 218.

[52] *Beauparlant v. Board of Trustees of Separate School Section No. 1 of Appleby,*
supra note 16.

occur. Teachers can easily avoid such findings without cancelling all field trips.

Parental Permission

Parental permission should always be obtained before embarking on a field trip. In some cases it is necessary for insurance coverage, and, in any event, parents have a right to be consulted on such matters. Parental consent forms should be easy to read and, where necessary, explained to the parents. If the outing is likely to be a long one, the consent form should be detailed and include a consent to necessary medical treatment.

The legal protection afforded by parental consent forms is minimal. It has been held that parents cannot sign away their children's independent right to sue,[53] and with respect to parents, courts are reluctant to construe a waiver of liability as applying to negligence. The parental consents in *Moddejonge*[54] did not prevent a lawsuit on behalf of the victims.

It has been suggested, however, that permission forms may be effective to prevent a prosecution for criminal negligence.[55] One cannot contract out of criminal responsibility, but, as a matter of evidence, parental consents reduce the chances of a factual finding of criminal negligence. Indeed, consents are good evidence that any foreseeable risks were overlooked by the parents as well as the teachers.

Even in cases of civil negligence, signed permission forms may provide a *prima facie* indication that the parents considered the activities listed therein suitable for their children. Since teachers' negligence is determined almost always by applying the careful-parent test, the accumulation of a sheaf of permission forms evidencing unanimous parental approval of the planned activities may provide a hedge against a suit alleging their inappropriateness. This would not be the case, of course, were an accident

---

[53] See *DeKoning and DeKoning v. Boychuk* (1951), 2 WWR (NS) 251 (Alta. SC), and *Stevens v. Howlitt* (1969), 4 DLR (3d) 50 (Ont. HC), as cited in J.C. Anderson, "School Board Negligence—An Update," in J. Balderson and J. Kolmes, eds., *Legal Issues in Canadian Education: Proceedings of the 1982 Canadian School Executive Conference* (Edmonton: Canadian School Executive, 1983), 121-22.

[54] *Moddejonge v. Huron County Board of Education*, supra note 14.

[55] See A.M. Thomas, *Accidents Will Happen: An Inquiry into the Legal Liability of Teachers and School Boards* (Toronto: OISE Press, 1976), as cited by Community Legal Education Ontario, *Legal Responsibility to Students* (Toronto: CLEO Press, 1979), 26.

to happen in the course of any activities that deviated from the approved list.

Whether students themselves can contractually waive their right to sue a school board for negligence by signing a release form is a complex question. Where the student has reached the age of majority, the question will turn on whether the content and form of the release give adequate information and notice to the student concerning the nature of the risks and the fact that, should an injury occur, he or she assumes all legal responsibility.[56] However, where the student is still a minor (usually, under 18 years of age), the common law of infants' contracts provides the answer. In general, contracts made by minors are either void or voidable by the infant upon attaining the age of majority. An exception exists in the case of contracts for necessaries, which can be enforced against minors. Necessaries include food, clothing, shelter, and, possibly, education. The possible inclusion of education as a necessary has led some commentators to conclude that minors can therefore enter a binding contract waiving their right to sue for the negligent provision of educationally related services—for example, extracurricular activities and field trips.[57] However, even in the case of contracts for necessaries, the courts have held that the contract must be for the benefit of the contracting minor. A problem therefore exists in the case of contracts permitting participation in activities only if the student promises to waive his or her right to sue for negligence, since such contracts arguably have both advantages and disadvantages for the contracting student. It appears, however, that the courts will be prepared to construe these types of contracts as void for containing terms that could only be seen as being to the minor's detriment. Thus, in *Miller v. Smith and Co.*,[58] the court ruled void a term in a minor's contract of employment that attempted to limit the minor's compensation for injury resulting from the employer's negligence. The court relied on *Beam v. Beatty*,[59] in which the court held that an infant could not contract himself out of secured rights or subject himself to a penalty. In short, it appears that an infant cannot enter a contract containing stipulations that must be to his or her disadvantage, and, further, that courts will construe contracts releasing infants' rights to be in that category.

---

[56] See the discussion of voluntary assumption of risk in chapter 4.

[57] See W.H. Giles, *Schools and Students* (Toronto: Carswell, 1988), at 132.

[58] *Miller v. Smith and Co.*, [1925] 3 DLR 251 (Sask. CA).

[59] *Beam v. Beatty* (1902), 4 OLR 554 (CA).

As a practical matter, many parents are deterred by parental consents from bringing legal action. This is because they are often poorly informed about their legal rights and have neither the time nor the money to consult a lawyer. As a matter of ethics, it seems distasteful that a school board should take advantage of the ignorance or poverty of parents. Parental consents should be accepted for what they are—useful evidence in court and a means of keeping parents informed. Also, if drafted carefully, a parental permission form could contain an effective waiver of the parents' right to sue for any damages they themselves might incur as a result of an injury to their child. Moreover, parents could be asked to indemnify teachers for any claim that their child might make as a result of a field trip. Again, whether school boards should qualify the opportunity of students to participate in extracurricular activities by requiring their parents to waive their right to sue for negligence and even to agree to indemnify the board for successful student claims, is an ethical question for each board to weigh and determine.

Even in cases where the students are adults, it should not be assumed that the courts will readily find them to have consented to high-risk activities. In *Bain*, while the court found the 19-year-old plaintiff to have assumed some of the *physical* risks of mountain climbing, it did not find that he had assumed the *legal* risks involved.[60] By permitting the activity, the teacher had made it an "approved" one, implying the board's retention of legal responsibility.

Safe Premises and Equipment

Statutory Duties

Under most provincial education statutes a school board is required to keep both its premises and equipment in a safe condition. There may also be a corresponding legislative duty to inspect premises and equipment regularly.[61]

Courts have held boards to their statutory duties. As pointed out earlier, however, unless a statute explicitly provides a cause of action in damages for breach of its prescribed duties, courts will rarely award damages for mere failure to fulfill a statutory

---

[60] See also the discussion under the heading "Voluntary Assumption of Risk," in chapter 4.

[61] For example, see the Ontario Education Act, RSO 1990, c. E.2, ss. 170(8) and 265(i)(j), and RRO 1990, reg. 298, s. 11(3)(l).

duty. However, the omission in question may well provide strong evidence of a breach of the defendant's common law duty of care.

Boivin v. Clenavon School District[62] involved a grade 4 student who fell from hanging ladders in the playroom onto a cement floor. The statute and regulations required the board to provide sporting equipment and properly maintain it; the critical question was whether mats should have been provided for the floor. Taking account of the limited resources of the small rural school and the many years in which the ladders were safely used, the court concluded that the accident was not foreseeable and imposed no liability.

However, when a child was injured by the use of a faulty teeter-totter, the court found the school board liable.[63] In *Pook v. Ernesttown School Trustees*,[64] a 14-year-old boy was injured when he fell on some rubble in the schoolyard during a scuffle. Regulations made under the applicable education statute required that the school grounds be kept clean and neat. Another regulation required the board to give "assiduous attention to the health and comfort of the pupils." Relying on these provisions, the court held that the board was in breach of its duties to maintain safe premises.

Occupier's Liability

The General Framework

In addition to specific statutory duties regarding the provision of safe facilities, school boards also have duties as owners and occupiers of school properties. Liability as an occupier is set by statute in some provinces, such as Ontario, Manitoba, and British Columbia, and by common law in others, such as Nova Scotia. Occupier's liability is that area of the law that deals with the liability of an owner or occupier of land for injuries suffered by persons while on the land. As a branch of the law of negligence, occupier's liability requires consideration of the nature of the duty owed by the occupier or owner and whether that person met the standard imposed in a particular case.

---

[62] *Boivin v. Clenavon School District*, [1937] WWR 170 (Sask. CA).

[63] See *Schultz v. Crosswald School Trustees* (1930), 1 WWR 579 (Alta. SC).

[64] *Pook v. Ernesttown School Trustees*, [1944] 4 DLR 268 (Ont. HC).

In those provinces where occupier's liability law has not been codified and remains governed by the common law, the standard imposed on an occupier will depend on the characteristics of the person who entered the property. The courts have divided these persons into three different categories—invitees, licensees, and trespassers. An invitee is generally defined as a person who is on the property with the express or implied permission of the occupier and from whom the occupier stands to derive some economic advantage or benefit, such as a customer in a store.[65] A licensee is a person who is on the property with the express or implied permission of the occupier but from whom the occupier will not derive any economic advantage or benefit—for example, a friend paying a social visit. A trespasser is a person who is on the property without the permission of the occupier. The decision as to which category a person fits will determine the duty owed by the occupier; the obligation to take steps to avoid injury is highest with respect to an invitee and lowest with respect to a trespasser.[66]

Differing Standards

An occupier's duty to an invitee is to take reasonable care to protect the invitee from "unusual dangers" of which the occupier *is or ought to be aware.* An unusual danger is considered to be one that the invitee could not reasonably be expected to apprehend or discover for himself or herself. The effect of this rule is that the occupier has a positive duty to take reasonable steps to discover the existence of any hidden or unusual dangers and to take reasonable steps to prevent harm to an invitee. The category of invitee is the one most relevant to school boards.

An occupier's duty to a licensee is less than that owed to an invitee. There is no affirmative duty requiring inspection of the premises; however, the occupier must take reasonable steps to protect the licensee from any hidden dangers or conditions of which the occupier is *actually aware*. This distinction between the duties owed to invitees and licensees has been summarized by J.G. Fleming:

> The hallmark of an invitor's duty, as compared with that of a licensor, is that it extends not only to dangers which he knows,

---

[65] See A.M. Linden, *Canadian Tort Law*, 6th ed. (Toronto: Butterworths, 1997), at 641.

[66] For an excellent examination of the different categories of liability, see J.G. Fleming, supra note 7, at 417-50.

but also to those which he ought to know. In short he must
take affirmative steps to ascertain the existence of, and eliminate, perils that a reasonable inspection would disclose.[67]

If an occupier has knowledge of a dangerous condition that a
person using reasonable judgment and conduct in the circumstances would not expect, then the occupier has a duty to take
reasonable steps to protect the licensee.

An occupier's duty to a trespasser is minimal; essentially, it is
limited to the obligation not to create deliberately an unsafe condition so as to injure or harm the trespasser. This has often been
described as a duty of "common humanity," which includes, for
example, not setting traps for people. Fleming suggests that the
character of the intruder is an important factor and expressly
refers to the position of children.

> "A wandering child or a straying adult stands in a different
> position from a poacher or a burglar. You may expect a child
> when you may not expect a burglar." Especially allurements
> to little children, although no longer constituting an inde-
> pendent ground for converting their status to that of a licen-
> see, may greatly increase the chance of them coming hither.[68]

In recent years the harsh treatment traditionally afforded trespassers under occupier's liability law has been somewhat softened.[69]

The School Context

There is some uncertainty about the standard of care required of
school authorities with respect to the protection of students from
harm due to hazardous conditions on the school premises. The
prevalent view appears to be that the duty of care owed by school
authorities to students is the same as that owed to invitees. The
rationale for this classification was expressed by the Ontario Court
of Appeal in *Portelance v. Board of Trustees of Roman Catholic
Separate School for School Section No. 5*:

> Inasmuch as pupils enter school premises not as mere volun-
> teers or as a matter of grace, but in accordance with a statu-
> tory right and duty, they enter "on business which concerns
> the occupier and upon his invitation, express or implied." Thus

---

[67] Supra note 7, at 430.
[68] Ibid., at 444.
[69] Ibid., at 440-46.

they are in the same position as persons who enter premises as of right, i.e., as invitees.[70]

Other courts have decided that the duty of care owed to students is higher than that owed to a regular invitee.[71] In *Ellis v. Board of Trustees for Moose Jaw Public School District et al.*, the school board and a private contractor were held liable for the damages suffered by a grade 7 student injured on school property. The contractor was installing new roofing materials on the school and was using a pulley to raise the materials to the roof. A group of students were in the habit of climbing up and swinging on the ropes to the pulley. On one occasion this resulted in the equipment being pulled down and striking a student. In deciding that the higher standard of care was applicable, the court made the following comment:

> In this case it seems to me that in view of the duty of supervision which the law imposes upon school authorities more specific care is demanded of them than that which is ordinarily required from the occupier of premises in respect of invitees thereon.[72]

The difficulty with this approach is that it takes two essentially distinct concepts—the principle of occupier's liability and the duty of school authorities to supervise students—and attempts to combine them within the framework of occupier's liability alone. Such a combination does not seem appropriate. The issue of whether school authorities have breached their duty to inspect the premises and ensure that they are safe and the issue of whether they have breached their duty to provide adequate supervision for students are two different matters. It is more appropriate to continue to treat them separately.[73]

---

[70] *Portelance v. Board of Trustees of Roman Catholic Separate School for School Section No. 5* (1962), 32 DLR (2d) 337 (Ont. CA), at 340. For other decisions indicating that students are to be treated as invitees, see *Sombach v. Board of Trustees of Regina Roman Catholic Separate High School District of Saskatchewan* (1969), 9 DLR (3d) 707 (Sask. QB), and *Phillips v. Regina Public School District Number 4* (1976), 1 CCLT 197 (Sask. QB).

[71] See *Ellis v. Board of Trustees for Moose Jaw Public School District and Blondin Roofing Products Limited*, supra note 25, and *Cropp v. Potashville School Unit No. 23* (1977), 81 DLR (3d) 115 (Sask. QB).

[72] *Ellis*, supra note 25, at 27.

[73] For criticism of the imposition of a higher standard of care owed to students than that owed to invitees, see John Barnes, "Annotation on *Cropp v. Potashville School Unit No. 23*" (1977), 4 CCLT 12.

One case that adopted this separate method of analysis was the Ontario Court of Appeal decision in *Portelance*.[74] A group of 12-year-old students were playing tag at noon. During the course of the game, two boys ran into an area of thick hawthorn trees; they were struck in the eyes by branches and blinded. Having decided that the applicable duty was that owed to an invitee, the court considered whether the hawthorn trees were an "unusual danger" and held that they were not, because 12-year-old boys should know better than to run into thick bushes. The court then went on to decide whether the system of supervision provided by the school was adequate.

Since the applicable duty of care owed to students is equivalent to that owed to an invitee, the next question that arises is what constitutes an "unusual danger" from which the students are entitled to be protected. In determining whether a danger is unusual a court will consider the general characteristics of the class of persons to whom the duty is owed. Therefore, as in *Portelance*, it is relevant to note whether the students are familiar with the school property. Another factor is the age of the students; in *Portelance* the court observed that 12-year-old boys should have been aware that their behaviour might cause them harm.

In the case of *Sombach v. Board of Trustees of Regina Roman Catholic Separate High School District of Saskatchewan*,[75] a 14-year-old high school student, in a rush to join her teammates on the way to a volleyball tournament, mistakenly walked through an unmarked glass panel beside an open front door. The school authorities were aware of the potential danger of these panels; in the past they had taken steps to make them visible by sandblasting patterns or hanging strips of paper on them. The court held that these panels presented an unusual danger and that the school authorities were liable because they had not taken proper steps to make the particular panel visible.

In *Phillips v. Regina Public School District No. 4*,[76] it was held that ice on a school sidewalk is an unusual danger that may give rise to school board liability if a student slips. In *Phillips*, the injured student was 18 years old; the court decided that she had not been exercising proper care for her own safety, and therefore reduced the amount of damages recovered according to the doctrine

---

[74] Supra note 70.

[75] Ibid.

[76] *Phillips v. Regina Public School District No. 4* (1976), 1 CCLT 197 (Sask. QB).

of contributory negligence, discussed in chapter 4. In another example of a relatively ordinary situation giving rise to occupier's liability, a temporary sidewalk made of large pieces of crushed rock produced an unstable footing that resulted in a 14-year-old student stumbling and injuring himself.[77]

Items that have been classified as not sufficiently dangerous to give rise to liability are a stone wall[78] and a piece of wire.[79] In *Durham v. Public School Board of North Oxford*, an 11-year-old student was injured while playing with a piece of bent wire that he found on school property. The court held that the wire was not inherently dangerous but became dangerous only through mischance or misadventure.

As the preceding cases indicate, most of the conditions that have been held to be "unusual dangers" are relatively common. This indicates that prudent school authorities should establish a system of regular inspection and maintenance of school property and correct any hazardous conditions without delay. School boards should be clear in assigning the responsibility to a particular employee, whether it be the school janitor or the principal.

When students are on school property outside normal school hours, the duty owed to them will depend on the reason for their presence on the property. If they are attending a school-sponsored event, such as a basketball game or a dance, they probably will be classified as invitees, and the school authorities owe the corresponding duty. If they are not at a school-sponsored event, they probably will be classified as licensees; the duty then owed by the school authorities will extend only to protecting the students from any hidden or concealed dangers of which the authorities are actually aware.

In *Sombach*, a student walked through a glass panel after school hours while preparing to attend a school volleyball game. The court had no difficulty in holding that the school authorities owed the same duty of care to the student as to an invitee. In another case, an 18-year-old student at a private boarding school was injured by a defective electric lamp in the dormitory.[80] Although

---

[77] See *Cropp v. Potashville School Unit No. 23*, supra note 71.

[78] See *Ward v. Hertfordshire County Council*, [1970] 1 All ER 535 (CA).

[79] See *Durham v. Public School Board of North Oxford* (1960), 23 DLR (2d) 711 (Ont. CA).

[80] *Scrimgeour v. Board of Management of Canadian District of the American Lutheran Church*, [1947] 1 DLR 677 (Sask. CA).

the accident occurred outside school hours, the court held that the school owed the student the duty of care owed to an invitee. The school was not liable because the defect could only have been discovered by dismantling the lamp or by testing it with electrical instruments. The court felt that it would place an unreasonable burden on school authorities to require them to inspect all lamps on a daily or weekly basis.

In *Boryszko et al. v. Board of Education of City of Toronto*,[81] it was held that a pile of building blocks left on the property by a contractor was not converted into a trap by virtue of the conduct of an unidentified boy who was knocking blocks off the pile, one of which struck and injured the plaintiff. When students return to school property in the evening simply to play, their status is that of a licensee; they probably would not be classified as trespassers because, in the absence of express directions to the contrary, school authorities will be said to have given an implied consent to the use of the school playground outside school hours. However, if students were to break into the school building itself, they undoubtedly would be classified as trespassers, not as licensees. The duty owed to licensees is to protect them from any concealed dangers or traps of which the school authorities are aware.

The duty owed to non-students similarly depends on the classification of the person entering the property. If the person is a parent attending the school for a school-related purpose, such as parent–teacher night or a school concert, he or she will probably be classified as an invitee.[82] In *Sanfacon v. Dartmouth School Board*,[83] an adult attending evening extension courses at a local high school was classified as an invitee.

The school grounds—for example, the playground or the athletic field—are generally available for public use; school authorities could be said to have implicitly consented to persons crossing the property or using the facilities outside school hours. In these cases, such persons will be classified as licensees. However, as noted above, it is doubtful that there is an implied consent to the presence of persons in the school buildings themselves outside school hours. Exceptions to this rule are specific functions, such

---

[81] *Boryszko et al. v. Board of Education of City of Toronto* (1962), 35 DLR (2d) 529 (Ont. CA).

[82] See *Griffiths v. St Clements School*, [1938] 3 All ER 537 (KB), aff'd. [1941] AC 170 (HL).

[83] *Sanfacon v. Dartmouth School Board* (1977), 25 NSR (2d) 451 (NS SC).

as a school activity or a meeting of a group that has been given permission to use the school. In the latter case, the permission given may be limited to a specific area, such as a classroom. Therefore, if a member of the group goes outside the permissible area to another part of the school, such as the gymnasium, he or she may well be classified as a trespasser rather than a licensee. However, an occupier wishing to limit an invitee's use of the premises should do so in clear terms.[84]

Would a school board be liable for an injury that occurred in the evening on school premises used by the public and supervised voluntarily by one of the school's teachers? This was the issue in *Lataille v. Les Commissaires D'Écoles de la Municipalité Scolaire de Farnham et Mercier*,[85] in which an 11-year-old girl lost her eye when she was accidentally struck by a hockey stick. In ruling that the school board was not liable for the injury, Montgomery J of the Quebec Court of Appeal stated:

> In the present instance, the Commissioners had no duty to provide for the entertainment of the public or to make the school or any of its facilities available to the public outside of normal school hours. They merely tolerated its use, and I cannot see that their position is different from that of any private citizen who might permit children to play on his property. There is a duty upon a landowner who knows that children are using this property not to have any hidden dangers that might constitute a trap ([see] *Terres Noires Ltée. v. Tellier*, [1964] QB 535) but there was nothing inherently dangerous in the basement room. I cannot accept the proposition that merely because a person knows that children are regularly playing on his property, he is obliged to supervise them to ensure that one of them is not hurt by the actions of another child.[86]

The Court of Appeal's decision was upheld by the Supreme Court of Canada on appeal.[87] The *Lataille* case provides another example of how courts often confuse the duty of supervision and occupier's liability.

---

[84] See Fleming, supra note 7, at 441.

[85] *Lataille v. Les Commissaires D'Écoles de la Municipalité Scolaire de Farnham et Mercier* (1973), 9 NR 372 (Que. CA).

[86] Ibid., at 374.

[87] *Lataille v. Les Commissaires D'Écoles de la Municipalité Scolaire de Farnham et Mercier* (1975), 9 NR 368 (SCC).

Statutory Codification and Clarification

In some provinces, the obligations of owners and occupiers of premises have been simplified and expressed in statutory form. The Ontario Occupiers' Liability Act[88] is a good example. Statutory codification is a preferable approach to the problem and provides clearer guidance about questions of liability than the rather confusing common law scheme, which depends so heavily upon classifications. Statutory reform would be particularly helpful for schools, which do not easily fit the existing common law categories.

Under provincial occupier's liability legislation, the duty owed by occupiers is, generally, to take reasonable steps to see that persons entering the premises are reasonably safe. In a recent case from British Columbia,[89] where such legislation exists, a board was held liable when a parent fractured her knee after slipping on an icy entrance to the school. The failure of the school's custodian to keep the area free of the ice that lay under fresh snow constituted failure by the board to maintain its premises in a reasonably safe condition.

A similar result occurred in *Still v. St. James-Assiniboia School Division No. 2*.[90] In this case, a member of the public suffered a bad ankle fracture when he slipped on an icy patch while walking from the parking lot to the school where he was taking an evening course. The route the plaintiff had taken, although not a sidewalk, was obviously a path used by many students. The court rejected arguments that the plaintiff was at fault for not watching where he was walking because evidence showed that this area of the school grounds was improperly lit, making it impossible to determine where the sidewalk ended and the grass began. The Manitoba Occupiers' Liability Act[91] required that the school board take reasonable care in all circumstances to make its premises safe. It was reasonable for the plaintiff to expect that this area would be well lit, given its frequent use as a pathway. After finding that the board had breached its duty to make the pathway safe by salting, sanding, and providing adequate lighting, the court awarded the plaintiff approximately $65,000, including general

---

[88] Occupiers' Liability Act, RSO 1990, c. O.2.

[89] *Dias v. Board of School Trustees of School District No. 11 (Trail)*, [1986] BCJ no. 1296 (SC).

[90] *Still v. St. James-Assiniboia School Division No. 2* (1995), 103 Man. R (2d) 163 (QB).

[91] The Occupiers' Liability Act, RSM 1987, c. O8.

damages of $22,000. There is an obvious lesson to be learned from this case, beyond the reminder to keep premises well lit and free from ice. Boards must realize that their acquiescence in the use of their premises in unintended or even unauthorized ways will extend their duty of care to such uses.

A dilemma can thus arise for boards whose premises are receiving unauthorized and potentially hazardous use by members of the public. Occupiers who choose to warn entrants of possible hazards risk having such warnings interpreted as invitations to use the premises. In *Sorensen v. Frontenac Lennox and Addlington Roman Catholic Separate School Board*,[92] an Ontario court held that a board was not obliged to warn about the danger in descending a hill at one of its schools because doing so could be interpreted as an implied invitation, which would have been contrary to its policy against use of the hill. However, boards should not risk ambiguity but, in their policies and published and posted notices, should make it clear that certain uses of their premises are prohibited.

Occupiers may not be held responsible for the unauthorized use of premises where they took reasonable steps to preclude the usage in question, as in *Sall v. Board of School Trustees of School District 43 (Coquitlam)*.[93] In *Sall*, a former student suffered serious injuries when he fell off the roof of the school attempting to retrieve a ball during a game of wall-ball that he was playing with others in the schoolyard one evening. In denying the plaintiff recovery under the British Columbia Occupiers' Liability Act,[94] the BC Supreme Court held that the board's measures to prevent people from climbing onto the roof—namely, installing wire mesh barriers, greased rollers, and plywood sheets—satisfied its duty under the Act to see that a person using its premises was reasonably safe under all circumstances. The court remarked that the board was not the insurer of an entrant's safety and that the plaintiff had voluntarily assumed the risk of injury by using the premises in a way that he knew the school board had attempted to prevent.

Voluntary assumption of risk also defeated an occupier's liability suit by a 16-year-old student who broke his wrist after falling

---

[92] *Sorensen v. Frontenac Lennox and Addlington Roman Catholic Separate School Board* (1996), 7 OTC 296 (Gen. Div.).

[93] *Sall v. Board of School Trustees of School District 43 (Coquitlam)*, [1995] BCJ no. 50 (SC), aff'd. (1996), 31 BCLR (3d) 18 (CA).

[94] Occupiers' Liability Act, RSBC 1996, c. 337.

out of a tree he had climbed during a supervised ball game in the schoolyard.[95] However, relying on the courts to rule that student daredevils invariably assume the risks associated with their conduct is a dangerous practice. In cases where supervisors are present, the obvious question arises why they permitted a student to undertake such foolhardy conduct. Moreover, as we discuss in chapter 4, courts have traditionally been averse to dismissing negligence actions on the basis of a student's having voluntarily assumed the risk. They have much preferred to apportion fault by applying the doctrine of contributory negligence.

---

[95] *Catherwood v. Board of School Trustees, School District No. 22 (Vernon)*, [1996] BCJ no. 1373 (SC).

4

Defences and Limits to Negligence

Certain defences are open to teachers and school boards to refute a claim of negligence or to limit their liability. Defences based on territorial and temporal limitations have particular application to the school setting. We have already discussed in chapter 2 some of the problems inherent in imposing liability for accidents occurring before and after school hours. Defences based on the conduct of the plaintiff are more general in nature and will be only briefly examined in this book.[1]

Territorial Limitations

For the purposes of occupier's liability, a school board is liable only for premises that it occupies, but it is deemed to occupy all school property. Thus, in *Magnusson v. Board of Nipawin School Unit No. 61*,[2] the school board was not found liable when a student was injured by broken glass in an adjacent fairground. Note, however, that in some cities, the duty of occupiers is extended by city bylaws to include the removal of snow and ice from the sidewalks in front of their property.[3]

The school's duty to supervise, however, can extend beyond the immediate school grounds. In *Magnusson*, the court held that the proper standard of supervision did not necessitate a fence to prevent students from straying onto the fair grounds. It emphasized that the standard was that of the careful parent, and, if there were inherently dangerous objects or allurements on property adjacent to the school grounds, greater precautions would be necessary;

---

[1] For more detail on the concepts of contributory negligence and voluntary assumption of risk, consult A.M. Linden, *Canadian Tort Law*, 6th ed. (Toronto: Butterworths, 1997), 453-94.

[2] *Magnusson v. Board of Nipawin School Unit No. 61* (1975), 60 DLR (3d) 572 (Sask. CA).

[3] See *Cummerford v. Board of School Commissioners of Halifax*, [1950] 2 DLR 207 (NS SC).

if a fair were in progress, even more stringent supervision would be required.

Pearson v. Vancouver Board of School Trustees[4] held that a school board's liability is limited to negligence that occurs on school grounds. When a student was involved in a bicycle accident 8 to 10 feet outside the school boundary, no liability was imposed on the school. The court held that there was no territorial "sea of jurisdiction" around the school property. The decision in *Pearson* is questionable; surely the "careful parent" does not abandon his or her responsibility to supervise when a child steps beyond his own property line. Risks may well be more foreseeable on the street in front of the school than on the school grounds; there should be no precise territorial limits on the duty of supervision. Of course, if a child walks home from school the school board is rarely responsible for accidents that may occur on the way.[5] Even then, however, the age of the child or special circumstances—for example, a winter storm—might impose a duty of supervision on the school.[6]

Statutory Limitations

Some education statutes contain express exemptions from school-board liability. Prince Edward Island and British Columbia exempt employees and board members from personal liability for the operation of school patrols and provide some protections for the board in other situations.[7] General exemptions from liability for both teachers and school boards are also found in Manitoba's, Saskatchewan's, and Prince Edward Island's education acts.[8] The education statutes in the other provinces appear to be silent on limitations.

---

[4] *Pearson v. Vancouver Board of School Trustees*, [1941] 3 WWR 874 (BC SC). The court's comments on the extent of school jurisdiction were *obiter dicta*; the main ruling was that there was no negligence.

[5] See *Edmonson v. Board of Trustees for Moose Jaw School District No. 1* (1920), 55 DLR 563 (Sask. CA).

[6] See the discussion of spatial and temporal limitations on the duty of care in chapter 2, under the headings "Before School Begins" and "After School Ends."

[7] School Act, RSPEI 1988, c. S-2.1, s. 120, and School Act, RSBC 1996, c. 412, ss. 94-95.

[8] Public Schools Act, RSM 1987, c. P250, ss. 86-89, Education Act, 1995, SS 1995, c. E-0.2, s. 232 and RSPEI 1988, c. S-2.1, s. 62. However, in *Thompson v. Board of Education of Eston-Elrose School Division No. 33 and Gorham*, [1997] SJ no. 158 (QB), the court construed s. 232(1) of the Saskatchewan Education Act to protect only a supervising teacher and not the school board from liability.

Statutes often place time limitations on the bringing of an action for intentional wrongs, negligence, and other civil causes. The exact time periods may differ from province to province and sometimes even within a province. The allowable time for bringing an action also depends on whether the claim is based on negligence, an intentional tort, a breach of contract, or some other ground. No matter how valid the claim, there will be no redress if the aggrieved person fails to launch a legal action within the time specified by the relevant statute.

Some provinces have a complicated patchwork of legislation controlling the law of limitations. For example, in Nova Scotia, the general statute governing such matters is the Limitations of Actions Act,[9] but there are other statutes that may be relevant, such as the Towns Act[10] or the Municipal Act.[11] Under the latter statutes, actions against towns or municipalities must be commenced within one year. These provisions are harsher than the normal limitation period for negligence actions in Nova Scotia, which is six years. Lawsuits against the Halifax and Dartmouth school boards must be brought within six months and one year respectively, and special notice must be given to the defendant.[12] It is important to note that for a child below the age of majority (usually age 18), the limitation period begins to run only when the age of majority is reached.[13]

Ontario has a single public-authorities protection statute.[14] This kind of statute provides a more coherent scheme, but is not without problems. It involves a determination of which acts are public in nature and which are private. Only public acts are subject to the time limitations of the statute. In Ontario, the dismissal of a teacher[15] and the moving of a piano by a janitor[16] have been found to be public acts.

---

[9] Limitations of Actions Act, RSNS 1989, c. 258, as amended.

[10] Towns Act, RSNS 1989, c. 472, as amended.

[11] Municipal Act, RSNS 1989, c. 295, as amended.

[12] See the City of Halifax Charter, SNS 1963, c. 52, s. 569, and the City of Dartmouth Charter, SNS 1978, c. 43A, s. 442, both as amended from time to time.

[13] See *Papamonopoulos v. Board of Education for the City of Toronto* (1986), 56 OR (2d) 1 (CA).

[14] Public Authorities Protection Act, RSO 1990, c. P.38.

[15] See *Stewart v. Lincoln Board of Education* (1972), 8 OR (2d) 168 (HC).

[16] See *Moffatt v. Dufferin County Board of Education*, [1973] 1 OR 351 (CA).

The classic case on distinguishing public from private actions is *McGonegal v. Gray*,[17] where a student was injured while lighting a stove in order to heat soup for lunch. The school did have an established lunch program, but on this particular day only the teacher wanted soup. In order for the act to be public and thus protected by the limitation, it had to be done pursuant to a "statutory or other public duty," according to section 11 (now section 7) of the Public Authorities Protection Act. The majority of the court found the act to be private, since the soup was being prepared for the teacher, but, somewhat paradoxically, did accept that the teacher's actions were in "the course of employment." The dissenting judges took a broader view of the statutory duties, and described the teacher's actions as public. The majority judges' desire to preserve the plaintiff's cause of action and to ensure that damages, if awarded, would be payable by the insured school board, is obvious in their reasoning in the case.

McGonegal v. Gray was applied in a somewhat surprising fashion in *Phelps v. Scarborough Board of Education*,[18] a case involving injury to a high school baseball player resulting from alleged lack of repair of the baseball diamond. As part of its defence, the board claimed that the plaintiff's action was statute-barred, because it had not been instituted within the six-month period required under the Public Authorities Protection Act. Following *McGonegal*, however, the court held that the limitation period in the Act applied only to public aspects of the board's duties, and that the maintenance of the ball field was a matter of internal administration or operations and, thus, a private aspect of its duties. Since, in Ontario, school boards are explicitly required by the Education Act to keep school premises in proper repair, it seems perverse that the repair of a playing field would be construed to be a private rather than a public matter. In any event, the court's ruling on this issue was merely *obiter dicta* since the field was not found to have been in disrepair.

If there is a "continuance of injury or damage," then the six-month limitation period begins upon the completion of the continued wrongful action—for example, a continuous escape of radiation from a microwave oven. It has been held that the "continuance" phrase applies not to the continuing of the injuries themselves, but rather to the actions that caused them.[19] This

---

[17] *McGonegal v. Gray*, [1952] 2 SCR 274.

[18] *Phelps v. Scarborough Board of Education*, [1993] OJ no. 1318 (Gen. Div.).

[19] See *Ihnat v. Jenkins*, [1972] 3 OR 629 (CA).

Ontario ruling has been followed in Newfoundland, which has similar statutory language.[20] Because statutes of limitation are complex and subject to frequent amendments, it is wise to consult a lawyer soon after an accident if legal action is contemplated or expected.

Voluntary Assumption of Risk

Definition

A plaintiff can be said to have consented to the commission of a tort, whether intentional or negligence. There can be no consent to a crime, however, which is a wrong against the state as well as the individual. Voluntary assumption of risk by the plaintiff is a complete defence to negligence, and must be proved by the defendant. The defence of *volenti*, as it is often called, may arise either by an express agreement on the part of the plaintiff to assume the risk or by implication from the conduct of the parties. Courts have been reluctant to imply *volenti*, however, and even where there is an express agreement, they have been reluctant to imply consent to negligence; this point is illustrated in the discussion of parental permissions for field trips in chapter 3.

One case in which the defence of *volenti* was narrowly construed by the courts is *Car and General Insurance Company and Seymour v. Maloney*.[21] A 19-year-old waitress accepted a ride with a person whom she met in the restaurant. On the first day of the journey the driver consumed almost two bottles of rum while driving, and then stopped for the night. After breakfast the next morning the driver obtained more alcohol and set out with his passenger again. Ignoring suggestions that he allow his brother to drive, the driver continued to drink and had an accident in which the passenger was injured.

At trial, the court accepted the defence of *volenti*, but on appeal, the Supreme Court of Canada rejected it. In essence, the Supreme court held that although the injured passenger may have consented to certain risks, she did not agree to exempt the defendant from liability. It is not enough to show that certain risks were voluntarily assumed; one must also show that legal

---

[20] See *Colbourne v. Labrador East Integrated School Board* (1980), 27 Nfld. & PEI Rep. 376 (Nfld. SC).

[21] *Car and General Insurance Company and Seymour v. Maloney*, [1956] SCR 322.

liability for the loss was accepted. Given this narrow definition of the defence of *volenti*, which has been followed in later cases,[22] it is hard to imagine many situations in which the defence would be applied, especially to children. On rare occasions, however, the defence has figured into school negligence cases.

School Applications

A defence of *volenti* is often raised when injuries occur in sports contests. Both spectators and participants have been held to consent to the normal risks of the game, but not to unusual or abnormal risks.[23] In *Myers et al. v. Peel County Board of Education et al.*,[24] the student was not held to have accepted the legal risk associated with performing on the rings. Because he was entitled to expect that adequate matting was provided, he accepted the physical but not the legal risk. Before a person can legally consent to the risk he or she must be fully apprised of the nature of the risk. This makes it even more difficult to apply the defence in respect to young students. In *Dziwenka v. Regina*,[25] there was no suggestion that the disabled student using an unguarded circular saw assumed the risk; but an older child without a disability was barred from recovery on the basis of *volenti* on almost identical facts.[26]

The recent Ontario Court of Appeal decision in *Thomas v. Board of Education of the City of Hamilton*[27] illustrates the distinction between consenting to physical as opposed to legal risks. In *Thomas*, the plaintiff suffered a serious neck injury during a high school football game. The court found that the plaintiff and his mother had consented to all the normal risks of the game but not to negligent conduct on the part of the board or its employees.

---

[22] See *Miller v. Decker*, [1957] SCR 624, where an agreement to accept liability was found based on the active encouragement of the plaintiff, and *Lehnert v. Stein*, [1963] SCR 38, where the court reaffirmed that there must be acceptance of the legal as well as the physical risk.

[23] See *Agar v. Canning* (1965), 54 WWR 302 (Man. QB).

[24] *Myers et al. v. Peel County Board of Education et al.* (1977), 2 CCLT 269 (Ont. HC).

[25] *Dziwenka v. Regina*, [1972] SCR 419.

[26] It should be noted that this case predates the Supreme Court's narrowing of the defence of *volenti* in *Maloney*, supra note 22.

[27] *Thomas v. Board of Education of the City of Hamilton* (1994), 20 OR (3d) 598 (CA).

The appellant participated ... of his own free will. He was aware of the risk of injury, even serious injury, that is inherent to [sic] participation in a contact sport such as football. However, *he did not, through his consent to participate (and that of his mother), assume all risk of injury to the extent that the school authorities were relieved of the duty of care that they owed to him.* [Emphasis added.][28]

It would take a rather exceptional set of facts for a court to agree that a student had accepted the legal risk of injury and effectively released a board from liability. Attempts by boards to obtain evidence of such consent by requiring pupils and their parents to sign waivers are usually futile, for reasons discussed in chapter 3.

Contributory Negligence

While a successful *volenti* defence is rare, a finding of contributory negligence on the part of the plaintiff is far more common. Contributory negligence is negligence on the part of the plaintiff that led to the accident. At one time, a finding of contributory negligence was a complete bar to recovery, but now it merely reduces the claim for damages in proportion to the fault of the plaintiff. This undoubtedly explains why courts seem to prefer the defence of contributory negligence over that of *volenti*, which operates as a complete bar to recovery. The ability to apportion fault arguably permits courts to arrive at more equitable decisions. In most provinces, if the court cannot apportion the negligence, the question is settled by statute. For example, if degrees of fault cannot be established, some statutes[29] apportion liability equally between plaintiff and defendant.

Teachers, Students, and Parents

There is no doubt that adults can be contributorily negligent. In an Australian case, a teacher at a school for the mentally retarded tripped over a wire while pursuing a child on the playground. The court found 20 percent liability on the part of the

---

[28] Ibid., at 619.

[29] See, for example, Contributory Negligence Act, RSNS 1989, c. 95, s. 3, and Negligence Act, RSO 1990, c. N.1, s.4.

teacher, who should have seen the wire.[30] The situation of students is not so clear. The 14-year-old schoolgirl in *Sombach v. Board of Trustees of Regina Roman Catholic Separate High School District of Saskatchewan*[31] was held not to have been contributorily negligent in walking into glass doors at her school.

In *Eyres v. Gillis and Warren Ltd.*,[32] relying on the so-called rule of seven, the court stated clearly that no 6-year-old child could be contributorily negligent. This categorical age cut-off was later rejected by the Supreme Court of Canada in *McEllistrum v. Etches*,[33] where Kerwin J made the following statement:

> It should now be laid down where the age is not such as to make a discussion of contributory negligence absurd, it is a question for the jury in each case, whether the infant exercised the care to be expected from a child of like age, intelligence and experience.[34]

After *McEllistrum*, the way was clear for courts to address the question of contributory negligence of young children contextually rather than under a rigid age prescription. The *McEllistrum* test was used to deny a claim for contributory negligence in the case of an 8-year-old child with a mental age of three.[35] The test was also adopted in *Hoyt v. Hay and Board of School Trustees for District 20*,[36] where neither the grade-one child nor his parents were found contributorily negligent when the child was injured while crossing the road. The fact that the parents had instructed him on safety and had escorted him across the road in the past attested to the reasonableness of their actions. However, in *Dao v. Sabatino and Board of School Trustees (Vancouver)*,[37] the BC Court of Appeal made a finding of 50 percent contributory negligence against a 6-year-old plaintiff who, despite warnings from his parents and school about road safety, had run in front of a car

---

[30] *Hasaganic v. Minister of Education* (1973), 5 SASR 554 (SC).

[31] *Sombach v. Board of Trustees of Regina Roman Catholic Separate High School District of Saskatchewan* (1969), 9 DLR (3d) 707 (Sask. QB).

[32] See *Eyres v. Gillis and Warren Ltd.* (1940), 4 DLR 747 (Man. CA).

[33] *McEllistrum v. Etches*, [1956] SCR 785.

[34] Ibid., at 793.

[35] See *Finbow v. Domino* (1957-58), 23 WWR 97 (Man. QB).

[36] *Hoyt v. Hay and Board of School Trustees for District 20* (1978), 23 NBR (2d) 497 (QB).

[37] *Dao v. Sabatino and Board of School Trustees (Vancouver)* (1993), 16 CCLT (2d) 235 (BC SC).

while being walked home from school by his older sister. Some US cases have held that parents are not contributorily negligent in sending a 6-year-old child to school unattended.[38]

An interesting question arises in situations where parents' negligence *is* found to have contributed to an injury suffered by their child through the negligence of a third party. At one time, because a child was identified with the legal persona of his or her father, the parent's contributory negligence was imputed to the child, thus providing the defendant with a defence against the child's claim for damages. What J.G. Fleming describes as a "barbarous rule" that "visited the sins of fathers on off-springs"[39] has been abandoned by the courts. Now a parent's negligence that contributes to an injury to his or her child will serve only to reduce the parent's own claim for damages, if any, arising from the injury.

In sum, it is clear that courts view contributory negligence as a preferable alternative to the all-or-nothing defence of voluntary assumption of risk. Thus, in *Myers*,[40] although the court rejected the defence of *volenti*, it did find 20 percent contributory negligence on the part of the student. Performing a new manoeuvre on the rings without the presence of a spotter was held to constitute contributory negligence. When a student is simply following the orders of a teacher, however, it is more difficult to view his or her conduct as contributory negligence.[41] Like negligence itself, contributory negligence depends on the facts of each particular case.

---

[38] See, for example, *Meadors v. Gregory*, 484 SW 2d 860 (Ky. CA 1972).

[39] J.G. Fleming, *The Law of Torts*, 7th ed. (Sydney: The Law Book Company, 1987), 263-64.

[40] Supra note 24.

[41] See *Ramsay v. Larsen* (1964), ALR 1121 (Aust. HC). The finding of no contributory negligence may have been conditioned by the fact that contributory negligence is a complete bar to recovery in New South Wales.

5

Student and Parent Liability for Accidents

In some of the cases discussed in previous chapters, schools were found liable for torts committed by students against other students. Their liability was not based on any theory of vicarious responsibility, but rather on independent acts of negligence on the part of the school authorities. This section considers the liability of students and their parents for torts committed in schools.

Students

Contrary to popular belief, children, even very young children, are liable for their own tortious actions. The test is essentially that of "age, intelligence, and experience" discussed in the previous chapter on contributory negligence. In most cases, suing a child is not practical because he or she is unlikely to be insured for the loss or have the economic resources to cover it. There have been some such lawsuits in recent years, however. *McCue v. The Board of Education for the Borough of Etobicoke and Stewart*[1] is a good example. A grade 9 student was injured in the eye when another student shot a paper clip propelled by an elastic band. Both students were in a grade 9 science class at the time of the incident, and the teacher had not yet entered the classroom. Arguments that the school board, through its employees, was negligent in providing supervision failed. The court accepted the evidence of the teaching staff that an adequate system of supervision was in place, and rejected the evidence of a University of Toronto education professor who argued that greater precautions were needed. The professor's evidence was questioned on the basis that he had not taught in the schools for several years and was likely to be out of touch with the realities of the school situation. Having

---

[1] *McCue v. The Board of Education for the Borough of Etobicoke and Stewart,* an unreported decision of Carruthers J, September 24, 1982 (Ont. SC), summarized in J. Anderson, "Student Responsibility for Injury to Other Student" (1983), vol. 3, no. 4 *Canadian School Executive* 30.

absolved the school of liability, the court found the defendant student liable for negligence and his injured classmate contributorily negligent.

Intentional Torts

Whether a young child can commit an intentional tort, such as assault or battery, depends upon his or her capacity to form a legal intent. In *Tillander v. Gosselin*,[2] a 3-year-old child pulled another child of the same age out of her carriage and dragged her on the ground, producing a skull fracture and brain damage. The resulting lawsuit was dismissed because the court held that the defendant child did not intend the harm. The age of the child was the critical factor in reaching that conclusion. In a US case, a 4-year-old child was held to have the requisite intent for battery when she broke the arms of a babysitter.[3]

By the time that most children come to school they are likely capable of forming a legal intent to commit a tort. In the US case of *MacDonald v. Terrebonne Parish School Board*,[4] there was no question that the 10-year-old students in an educable mentally retarded class could commit intentional torts. In fact, the lawsuit was dismissed because the defendant student was found to have used reasonable force in self-defence against his aggressor. School-age children who are sued in tort can also raise the usual defences.

Another case involving an assault that resulted in an eye injury was *Bubner v. Stokes*.[5] The weapon in this case was a pen, thrown after the teacher had left the room. The students did not attend to their reading, as instructed, but caused a general commotion. There was evidence that the 9-year-old defendant intended to hit the plaintiff with the pen, and the court found that the lack of the specific intention to hit the child's eye was irrelevant. An argument that the plaintiff may have consented to the risk by engaging in earlier pen-throwing was rejected.

Clearly, students who are adults can, and will, be held liable for intentional torts committed on school premises. Even minor

[2] *Tillander v. Gosselin*, [1967] 1 OR 203 (HC).

[3] See *Ellis v. D'Angelo*, 253 P2d 675 (Cal. CA 1953).

[4] *MacDonald v. Terrebonne Parish School Board*, 253 So. 2d 558 (La. CA 1971).

[5] *Bubner v. Stokes* (1952), SASR 1 (Aust. SC).

scraps that begin consensually, can escalate and result in serious consequences for both participants, as *Walsh v. Buchanan*[6] illustrates. In this case, two 19-year-old grade 13 students with no prior disciplinary records began shoving and punching each other during a floor hockey game in the gym. The referee ejected both students from the game and sent them to the change rooms. Later, in the hallway, the students began a consensual fight that was witnessed by a large crowd of their fellow students. Although the plaintiff, who was a trained champion boxer, threw the first punch, the defendant eventually gained the advantage and began to pummel the plaintiff's head and body, eventually breaking his nose and chipping his tooth.

In the plaintiff's action for assault, the court ruled that, while the plaintiff had begun the fight, the defendant had used excessive force defending himself. Each combatant was found 50 percent responsible for the plaintiff's injuries. In addition to physical injuries, the plaintiff had suffered a long-lasting post-traumatic depression. The court awarded damages of almost $500,000, half of which were payable by the defendant.

Most boards and schools today have instituted anti-violence and "zero tolerance" policies that strictly outlaw fighting. As part of boards' educational programs teaching non-violent resolution of disputes, the potentially devastating costs of violent behaviour should be impressed on students. There is probably no better case study for this purpose than *Walsh*.

Negligence

Children can be found liable for negligence, but they are generally held to a lower standard of care than adults in similar circumstances. However, children who engage in adult activities appear to be an exception to this rule.[7] The major test to be applied appears to be that of "age, intelligence, and experience," as enunciated in *McEllistrum v. Etches*.[8] The situation is the same as that of the child being considered contributorily negligent, except that the child is a defendant rather than a plaintiff.

[6] *Walsh v. Buchanan*, [1995] OJ no. 64 (Gen. Div.).

[7] See A.M. Linden, *Canadian Tort Law*, 6th ed. (Toronto: Butterworths, 1997), 136-42, for a comprehensive treatment of the tort liability of children.

[8] *McEllistrum v. Etches*, [1956] SCR 785.

Parents

This section will be concerned only with one aspect of a parent's responsibility for his or her children—namely, accidents related to school activities. Since teachers are held to the standard of the careful parent, much can be gleaned about the duties of a parent from the school cases discussed in chapter 2. Issues of parental liability have also arisen with respect to contributory negligence in cases such as *Hoyt v. Hay and Board of School Trustees for District 20.*[9]

Duties to the Child

Children rarely sue their parents, although such actions, formerly disallowed at common law, are now possible.[10] The relationship of parent and child gives rise to a duty to exercise reasonable care for the safety of the child. Included in this duty are the provision of proper supervision, the avoidance of unreasonable risks, and proper instruction about the dangers that a child might encounter. As with teachers, the standard is one of reasonableness and not perfection; it varies with the known propensities of the child, the age of the child, and a host of other factors identified in the cases discussed in this book. In *Carmarthenshire County Council v. Lewis*[11] the court showed a rather typical sympathy and understanding for the difficult task facing a parent.

Duration of Duty

A parent is not responsible for the safety of his or her children indefinitely. The problem of establishing a cut-off point lies in the uncertainty about when a child becomes a responsible and autonomous person. Until the child reaches this state of independence, parents are responsible for his or her safety and must also exercise rights on the child's behalf. The degree of supervision required decreases with the age of the child. As a practical matter, the parental duty to supervise often ends when the child

---

[9] *Hoyt v. Hay and Board of School Trustees for District 20* (1978), 23 NBR (2d) 497 (QB).

[10] See *Deziel v. Deziel*, [1953] 1 DLR 651 (Ont. SC). Family law reform legislation also provides for such suits—for example, see the Family Law Act, RSO 1990, c. F.3, s. 65.

[11] *Carmarthenshire County Council v. Lewis*, [1955] AC 549 (HL).

reaches 16 or 17. Although provincial statutes usually set the age of majority and accountability at 18, they do not determine the question of when a parent's duty of care ceases. Instead, the matter is left to the common law, thus depending on a variety of factors, including the child's attributes and state of actual dependency on his or her parents, as well as the nature and degree of parental involvement in the events leading up to an accident and injury.

Duty to Others

There is considerable confusion about the tort liability of parents for damages caused by their children to others.[12] In all provinces except Quebec, parents are not vicariously responsible for the torts of their children;[13] they are liable, however, for their own acts of negligence in respect to their children.[14] Thus, it is possible to sue parents, or other persons standing in their place, for damages inflicted by a child, but only if the responsible adults have committed some act of negligence, usually a failure to supervise the child reasonably. If a father gives a child a loaded gun and sends him or her to school with it, the father may be liable for any damages that result. Applying the standard of the careful parent, the court in *Carmarthenshire* found the school liable when a child ran into the street and caused the death of a truck driver. This finding was reached not because of any vicarious liability for the child's wrongful act but because the schoolyard gate was improperly secured by the teacher. Many parents do compensate for the damages caused by their children out of a sense of moral obligation. In law, however, such compensation is only necessary where the parent is also at fault.

Quebec's Civil Code

In Quebec, teachers and parents are held responsible for the torts of children who are under their care and control by virtue of the Quebec Civil Code, art. 1054, which reads:

---

[12] For a general discussion of parents' duty to control their children, see E.R. Alexander, "Tort Responsibility of Parents and Teachers for Damages Caused by Children" (1965), 16 *University of Toronto Law Journal* 165, and A.M. Linden, *Canadian Tort Law*, 6th ed. (Toronto: Butterworths, 1997), 130-32.

[13] See *Thibodeau v. Cheff* (1911), 24 OLR 214 (CA).

[14] See *Robertson v. Butler* (1985), 32 CCLT 208 (NS SC).

[Any person] is responsible not only for the damage caused by his own fault, but also for that caused by the fault of persons under his control and by things which he has under his care.

The person having parental authority is responsible for the damage caused by the child subject to such authority.

Tutors are responsible in like manner for their pupils. ...

Schoolmasters and artisans [are responsible] for the damage caused by their pupils or apprentices while under their care.

The responsibility attaches in the above cases only when the person subject to it fails to establish that he was unable to prevent the act which has caused the damage.

This provision was applied to the school setting in *O'Brien v. Procureur Général de Québec*,[15] where a student was injured by an explosion in a laboratory in a provincial trade school. The teacher was not in the room at the time of the explosion. The Supreme Court held that the action was not foreseeable and could not have been prevented by the teacher's presence. The court also held that staff regulations that were related to staff discipline did not create any rights vis-à-vis third parties. In Quebec, parents and teachers are required to rebut a presumption of responsibility.[16]

---

[15] *O'Brien v. Procureur Général de Québec*, [1961] SCR 184.

[16] See also Ontario's Family Law Act, RSO 1990, c. F.3, s. 68, which places a similar onus on parents to rebut a presumption of liability.

6

Risk Management: The Best Defence

Defending a lawsuit for negligence represents the epitome of a reactive approach toward educational policy. It is preferable for boards to adopt proactive measures to minimize the risk of accidents and injuries. One might argue that the best expedient is simply to view accidents as inevitable and *transfer* the risk by purchasing adequate insurance coverage—something that boards must generally do, in any event, under provincial legislation. Reliance on increasingly costly insurance, however, in addition to having an obvious impact on taxpayers' wallets, ignores boards' moral responsibility to protect children from harm, not merely compensate them after it occurs.

All boards should institute risk management policies and practices, and ensure that they are communicated to, taught to, and practised by teachers, coaches, and other employees, as well as students. Rather than simply controlling risk by transferring it to an insurer, boards must accept responsibility for taking active steps to reduce accidents and injuries. Although many sophisticated risk management systems exist, we propose a simple three-point model as a useful starting point for administrators, teachers, coaches, and others who seek to control risk in the school environment.[1]

Our model requires that principals, teachers, coaches, and any others who owe a duty of care to students ask themselves three broad questions before undertaking activities or creating policies where risk of injury is a concern.

---

[1] For a variation of this model and further discussion of risk management measures, see Report of the National Fitness Leadership Advisory Committee (NFLAC), *Legal Liability Considerations for the Fitness Leader* (Ottawa: Fitness Canada), 11-15. See also S. Goodman and I. McGregor, *Legal Liability and Risk Management: A Resource Manual* (Toronto: Risk Management Associates, 1993). Although aimed primarily at recreational leaders, both resources contain useful discussions and recommendations that are easily transferrable to school settings.

A Simplified Risk Management Model

Academic value of the activity

The magnitude   Practicability of
of the risk   precautions

What Are the Risks?

All risks reasonably associated with any proposed activity should be listed. Remember that the concept of risk has two dimensions: the risk of accident, and the risk of injury.

It is obvious that the greater the potential injury, the more one expects measures to reduce the risk of accident. Competence in any area of endeavour encompasses the ability to identify and assess accurately the consequences and risks associated with activities in that area. Conversely, an inability to do so implies incompetence and demonstrates that the person(s) involved should not be in charge of the activity in question.

What Can Be Done To Eliminate or Reduce the Risks?

Much of the time it is impossible to eliminate all risk of mishap and injury. As discussed in previous chapters, some school activities are inherently dangerous; others are only potentially dangerous. However, as part of their legal duty of care, it is incumbent upon educators to take reasonable steps to reduce risks. As stated above, professional competence implies the ability to identify and assess risk. It similarly implies a knowledge of how to reduce risk. This knowledge is often specialized, peculiar to a specific professional role, such as shop teacher, lab instructor, or coach.

Risk reduction measures are part of the expert knowledge base of professionals and include:

• following approved general practice;

• keeping up to date on the research relating to safe practices in one's field;

- acquiring and using newer or safer equipment;

- acquiring and using safety equipment—for example, goggles, machine guards, or protective matting;

- providing participants with prior instruction, warning, and progressive training;

- providing in-service training to supervisors to identify and control risk, and to give first aid;

- lowering the supervisor–participant ratio;

- providing a higher intensity of supervision; and

- conducting periodic risk-control audits.

Are the Benefits Worth the Risks?

The final and, in many ways, the essential question requires that the benefits and risks inherent in a given activity be weighed. Traditionally, the social usefulness of conduct resulting in an injury has been a relevant factor in assessing negligence. It is obvious that as the risk rises, one expects a corresponding rise in the worth of the activity. Hazardous school activities should be capable of readily being seen as worthwhile, which in the educational setting means fulfilling defined curricular or co-curricular objectives. As we have seen in our discussion of negligence cases, particularly those involving field trips, satisfying students' fun-seeking whims seldom, if ever, qualifies as worthwhile.

An assessment of risk and cost—both financial and human—could easily result in a decision to eliminate the risk by eliminating the activity. This is a perfectly legitimate policy response as long as it does not destroy the richness of students' education, because of unwarranted litigation paranoia or unwillingness to adopt the reasonable measures required to maintain a worthwhile activity. Although parents expect a safe school environment, they do not expect it at the cost of a rich educational experience. The challenge for educational policy makers is to manage risk while meeting society's and parents' expectations about educational quality and excellence—an all the more daunting task in times when school activities are more dangerous, yet human and financial resources more scarce.

7

Educational Malpractice

> We hear sometimes of an action for damages against the unqualified medical practitioner, who has deformed a broken limb in pretending to heal it. But what of the hundreds of thousands of minds that have been deformed for ever by the incapable pettifoggers who have pretended to form them!
>
> Charles Dickens
> *Nicholas Nickleby*

An Overview

With the possible exceptions of some physical education teachers, lab instructors, and shop teachers, educators have rarely been sued for the faulty performance of their main task—teaching. Courts have allowed recovery for broken bones, but not for "broken minds, psyches and expectations."[1]

Some parents, however, have attempted to use tort law, especially negligence suits, as a tool of accountability for the quality of education provided their children. These sorts of lawsuits have typically alleged a failure to teach certain basic skills, such as literacy and numeracy. Sometimes the cases include claims for failure to diagnose students' learning disabilities, incorrect diagnoses of such problems, or wrongful placement of children with special learning difficulties. W.F. Foster lists the following non-exhaustive circumstances that could precipitate a law suit for educational malpractice:

    1. failure to provide or maintain reasonably adequate instructional, orientation, and career counselling programs;

    2. failure to provide or maintain reasonably adequate academic instruction, supervision, guidance and counselling, and evaluation systems by which a student's progress is monitored;

---

[1] H.N. Janisch, "Education Malpractice: Legal Liability for Failure to Educate" (1980), 38 *Advocate* 491, at 491.

3. failure to provide or maintain means to identify and deal with exceptional students or to initiate appropriate action when such a student is identified;

4. failure to provide reasonably adequate, qualified, and competent staff, and to ensure their continued adequacy and competency;

5. misleading or failing to advise students as to their academic progress, level of achievement, or capabilities;

6. failure to maintain discipline in the classroom;

7. failure to assign reasonably adequate and appropriate academic materials; and

8. failure to adopt reasonably adequate and appropriate methods of instruction.[2]

Most educational malpractice suits have occurred in the United States. It would be comforting to think that the paucity of such cases in Canada indicates that all Canadian teachers are competent. Realistically, however, with the large number of teachers in Canada, a range of professional competency is to be expected, and the lower end of the range could well represent an unacceptably low level of professional performance. Parents sometimes argue that school boards have been intimidated by unions and threats of lawsuits into protecting incompetent teachers at the expense of students.[3] In contrast, many teachers would argue that provincial governments and school boards contribute to teacher incompetence by decreasing funding for education, cutting necessary supplies, increasing student–teacher ratios, and requiring teachers to teach not only subjects for which they are not qualified but also an increasing number of mentally and physically challenged students in regular classroom settings.[4]

---

[2] W.F. Foster, "Educational Malpractice: A Tort for the Untaught?" (1985), 19 *Univeristy of British Columbia Law Review* 161, at 171-72.

[3] "Children Come Last" (August 7, 1981), *The Globe and Mail.*

[4] Teachers in many provinces are certified as teachers, not as teachers of express subjects. Thus Canadian courts are likely to follow the US lead in holding that there is no board malpractice in requiring a Spanish teacher to teach a class of mentally challenged children: see *MacDonald v. Terrebonne Parish School Board*, 253 So. 2d 558 (La. CA 1971).

Failure To Educate

There have been very few, and no successful, cases in Canada involving a negligence claim against either a teacher or a school board for failure to educate. Neither have any successful claims been made in the United States, although the issue has been raised in several cases. One of the earliest was *Trustees of Columbia University v. Jacobsen,*[5] in which a student sued the university for misrepresentation and deceit in failing to live up to the lofty claims that promised to impart wisdom, among other virtues, set forth in its calendar. The student lost his case, but, as Janisch indicates, this is but one of a series of university cases, many of which were based on the existence of an implied contract between the student and the university.[6] Although the contract theory appears to have won acceptance at the university level,[7] and would certainly apply to private schools, it is much less plausible at the first two levels of public education. It is hard to argue that there is any contract between a school board, which is bound by statute to provide education, and a student, who is compelled by the same statute to attend school.

Two 1970 appellate court decisions, one in California and one in New York, left little doubt that plaintiffs seeking damages for negligent provision of educational services face an uphill, if not hopeless, struggle. In *Peter W. v. San Francisco Unified School District,*[8] a school board was sued for negligence for failure to educate. A high-school graduate who could read only at the grade 5 level after 12 years of education alleged negligence, misrepresentation, and breach of statute. He claimed loss of income as a result of his functional illiteracy. Not only did the court reject his claims, it also found that there was no duty to provide a minimum level of skill and thus no cause of action in negligence.

A duty of care was held to exist with respect to educational malpractice in *Donohue v. Copiague Union Free School District,*[9] where a student claimed damages for illiteracy that was manifested in his inability to fill out a job application. What the court gave with one hand, however, it quickly took away with the other. The

---

[5] *Trustees of Columbia University v. Jacobsen,* 148 A2d 63 (NJ SC 1959).

[6] Supra note 1.

[7] See *Wong v. Lakehead University,* [1991] OJ no. 1901 (Gen. Div.).

[8] *Peter W. v. San Francisco Unified School District,* 131 Cal. Rptr 854 (CA 1976).

[9] *Donohue v. Copiague Union Free School District,* 391 NE 2d 1352 (NY CA 1979).

court found that the plaintiff did not in this case, and could not in most cases, show either legally recognized damages or the necessary causal link between the student's "injury" and the education system. Even more damaging to such claims in the future was the ruling that, as a matter of policy, educational malpractice claims should not be entertained.

The public policy rationale adopted by the courts in the United States to support their rejection of educational malpractice claims had three primary focuses. First, the courts feared that allowing such lawsuits would cause a flood of complaints—many spurious—and place a tremendous burden on school districts' financial and human resources. Second, they predicted that such suits would stifle educational innovation. Fearing litigation, educators would be loath to adopt any innovative practices lest they failed, and would be prompted to stay with safer methods whose educational benefits, albeit modest, could be demonstrated. The courts believed, somewhat ironically, that such litigation paranoia could well have a retrogessive effect on the quality of teaching. Finally, the courts refused to be cast in the role of educational experts. They felt ill-equipped to fashion educational policy through their rulings, which necessarily would seem to vilify certain educational practices or theories while endorsing others. In their view, society had placed this responsibility in the hands of the politicians, administrators and educational experts running the school system, and parental and student dissatisfaction regarding the quality of education delivered in the schools should be dealt with through an internal administrative complaint process rather than the courts.

Misclassification

One area in which a US court has found malpractice is that of classification by a school psychologist. In the notorious case of *Hoffman v. Board of Education of City of New York*,[10] a boy who was wrongly classified as "retarded" spent a decade in classes for the mentally disabled. The original ruling in favour of the child was later overturned by the New York Court of Appeals which clearly deferred to the judgment of the school board.[11] The *Hoffman* decision represents the epitome of rigid adherence to precedent

---

[10] *Hoffman v. Board of Education of City of New York*, 410 NYS 2d 99 (1978).

[11] *Hoffman v. Board of Education of City of New York*, 406 NE 2d 317 (NY CA 1979).

resulting in a defendant's inability to recover damages that he justly deserved. That realization may well have led a Montana court in 1982 to accept a cause of action under similar facts, although the court still felt compelled to distinguish the circumstances in the case from the usual genre of educational malpractice and characterize them as a violation of a mandatory statutory duty.[12]

Another US case dealt with the reverse of the problem in *Hoffman*. In *Pierce v. Board of Education of the City of Chicago*,[13] a child and his mother sued the school board for keeping the child in a regular class rather than putting him in a special class for the learning-disabled. Damages were claimed for the emotional injury suffered from having to compete in the regular class. The child had been tested and diagnosed as learning-disabled by a private doctor. The mother informed the board of this diagnosis and requested a transfer. When the case was tried on its merits, the mother lost. The Illinois court held that there was neither a statutory nor a constitutional duty to place a child in a special education class, that the school board should determine who is eligible for special education classes, and that there was no cause of action.[14]

Despite these US court rulings, it is not unreasonable to think that school psychologists and guidance counsellors might be potential targets of malpractice litigation because of their specialized activities, such as testing and classification, which can have

---

[12] See *B.M. v. State*, 649 P2d 425 (Montana SC 1982). For a review of statutory obligations across Canada with regard to special education, see W.J. Smith and W.F. Foster, "Equal Educational Opportunity for Students with Disabilities in Canada: A Platform of Rights To Build On" (1993-94), 5 *Education and Law Journal* 193; W.J. Smith and W.F. Foster, "Educational Opportunity for Students with Disabilities in Canada: Beyond the Schoolhouse Door" (1993-94), 5 *Education and Law Journal* 305; and W.J. Smith and W.F. Foster, "Educational Opportunity for Students with Disabilities in Canada: How Far Have We Progressed?" (1997), 8 *Education and Law Journal* 183.

[13] *Pierce v. Board of Education of the City of Chicago*, 358 NE 2d 67 (Ill. SC 1976).

[14] *Pierce v. Board of Education of the City of Chicago*, 370 NE 2d 535 (Ill. CA 1977). This ruling effectively reversed the earlier decision cited above.

[15] See *E (a minor) v. Dorset County Council*, [1995] 3 All ER 353 (HL), at 392-94, where Lord Browne-Wilkinson found no reason to exclude a cause of action for alleged breach of duty of care in providing psychological services to a pupil. On the legal dimensions of the school psychologist's role, generally, see R. Kimmins, "An Examination of Legislation Relating to the Practice of School Psychology" (unpublished MA dissertation, Mount Saint Vincent University, Halifax, 1982) and L. Fischer and G. Sorenson, *School Law for Counselors, Psychologists, and Social Workers*, 2d ed. (New York: Longman, 1991).

a significant effect on the lives of students.[15] However, to date, there appears to have been no successful negligence suit for misclassification *per se* in the United States.

Like their US counterparts, Canadian courts have denied recovery of damages in tort for educational malpractice. In *Bales v. School District 23 (Central Okanagan)*,[16] a school board was sued by the parents of a mentally disabled student for negligence in placing him in a segregated school for children with disabilities. The BC Supreme Court ultimately dismissed the plaintiffs' claim because the evidence failed to disclose an injury in the tort sense. The court observed that the law of negligence existed to enforce a duty to act reasonably to avoid harm, not a duty to achieve the greatest possible benefit. The case is significant, first, because of the implied legal entitlement found by the court in the BC School Act to an education "which meets some basic educational standard," and, second, because of the inference that there is no reason in principle why educational malpractice suits in tort should not proceed.

A subsequent Ontario case, however, followed the US lead in rejecting the plaintiffs' entitlement to even bring such claims. In *Hicks v. Board of Education for the City of Etobicoke*,[17] a parent sued the school board for negligent categorization and placement of her son as an exceptional pupil. The plaintiff also alleged that the board had breached its statutory duty under the Education Act to provide proper instruction for her son. The suit sought damages for developmental harm, mental anguish, and embarrassment, as well as compensation for money spent to remediate her child's learning problems. O'Connell J refused to recognize educational malpractice as a viable cause of action and struck out the plaintiff's claim. In doing so, he remarked that there was no case authority in Canada that recognized educational malpractice as a tort and he was persuaded by the public policy arguments in the US cases that he ought not to create a precedent by allowing the claim in this case to proceed.

Gould v. Regina (East) School Division No. 77[18] is a more recent but similarly ill-fated attempt to sue a Canadian school authority

---

[16] *Bales v. School District 23 (Central Okanagan)* (1984), 54 BCLR 203 (SC).

[17] *Hicks v. Board of Education for the City of Etobicoke*, [1988] OJ no. 1900 (QL) (Dist. Ct.).

[18] *Gould v. Regina (East) School Division No. 77*, [1996] SJ no. 843 (QB).

for educational malpractice. In *Gould*, a 7-year-old student and her parents sued the school board and a specific teacher for alleged malpractice that occurred when the plaintiff was in the defendant teacher's grade 1 class. The plaintiffs' claim listed six categories of "unsatisfactory, inappropriate and objectionable" conduct by the teacher, including subjecting students to demeaning comments and ridicule; consistently speaking in an inappropriately loud voice; neglecting or refusing to respond to the student-plaintiff's concerns about inadequate instruction, thereby discouraging her further efforts; bullying and intimidating the plaintiff and other students; not positively reinforcing students; and refusing or neglecting any offers of assistance from outside the classroom. The claim further alleged that the teacher had failed to perform her statutory duties under the Education Act:

(a) by failing to diligently and faithfully teach the pupils in her charge ... ;

(b) by failing to plan and organize the learning activities of the class with due regard for individual differences and needs of the pupils ... ;

(c) by failing to maintain good order and consistent and even handed discipline in the classroom ... ;

(d) by failing to conduct and manage assigned functions in the instructional program in accordance with the educational policies of the Defendant Board ...

and [that she had] thoroughly failed to meet the standard of care expected to be met by a teacher in providing for the supervision and protection of students ... as that of a careful, caring and prudent parent, taking into account the age and degree of skill and training of the said infant Plaintiff and the competence and capacity of the said infant Plaintiff.[19]

For its part, the Board was alleged to have failed to abide by its own statutory obligations—namely, to exercise general supervision and control over the school to ensure its effective and efficient operation; to appropriately place and replace teachers; to investigate issues and disputes regarding relationships among students, parents, and teachers; to recognize the defendant-teacher's "incompetence and gross misconduct"; and to appoint a duly qualified teacher for the plaintiff-pupil.

---

[19] Ibid., at para. 8.

The parents had withdrawn their daughter from the school in question because of the alleged malpractice, which they claimed caused them "stress, anxiety and disruption in their home and community life and loss of schooling."

After reviewing several US and Canadian authorities, the court granted a motion for an order striking out the statement of claim as disclosing no reasonable cause of action. The court held that simply breaching statutory duties was not negligence *per se*. Moreover, even if the defendants were negligent in performing their duties under the Education Act, the statement of claim did not disclose compensable loss. Nervous shock must transcend mere grief or stress and be manifest as a recognizable psychiatric illness.

The court broached the public policy dimension of malpractice claims by discussing the inappropriateness of asking the court to set standards for classroom teachers. Matheson J stated that it was surely not the function of the courts to establish and supervise the maintenance of such standards.

If the court had stopped there, as most courts have in this kind of case, it would be easy to cast *Gould* as just another nail in the coffin of educational malpractice suits. However, the court went on to qualify its rejection of the claim by stating that

> [o]nly if the conduct is sufficiently egregious and offensive to community standards of acceptable fair play should the courts even consider entertaining any type of claim in the nature of educational malpractice.[20]

Thus, it seems open to would-be plaintiffs to argue in future cases that their facts fall within the exception established in *Gould* and it will be up to future courts to determine, in concrete terms, exactly what Matheson J had in mind.[21]

Although educational malpractice suits have routinely failed, suspicions linger that courts are not done forever with the idea of tort

---

[20] Ibid., at para. 47.

[21] The inference left in *Gould*, that some exceptional cases might succeed, did not apparently affect a BC Provincial Court judge who subsequently dismissed a malpractice suit alleging failure to teach the prescribed curriculum. In *Haynes v. Lleres et al.*, [1997] BCJ no. 1202 (Prov. Ct.), the court held that public policy grounds prevented such suits and that teachers should enjoy a broad discretion to teach as they see fit within a program's framework. It should also be noted that s. 94 of the School Act, RSBC 1996, c. 412, insulates educators from personal liability for negligent performance of their duties unless they have been "guilty of dishonesty, gross negligence or malicious or willful misconduct."

liability for the negligent provision of an education. Another broad hint that they are not came in a ruling by the British House of Lords in 1995.[22] The ruling concerned five cases involving plaintiffs who had sued public authorities for negligent performance of their statutory duties and vicarious liability for breach of the common law duties of care owed by their professional employees. In three of the cases, the defendants were education authorities who were sued for failure to diagnose or properly provide for students' special education needs. One student-plaintiff claimed that, had his dyslexia been properly diagnosed, appropriate remedial services would have been provided, leading in turn to an easing of his learning difficulties. The House of Lords was required to rule on whether the claims should be struck out for disclosing no recognized cause of action.

The Lords' decision has been described as a "mixed blessing" for public authorities.[23] Although they held that there could be no private law claim for damages for breach of a statutory duty, because there was no common law duty of care to perform a statutory duty carefully, the Law Lords did recognize the existence of a duty by public authorities to ensure that advice given by one of their service providers, such as psychological counsellors, is reasonable. Moreover, in *Christmas v. Hampshire County Council*,[24] the court appeared to suggest that there was no reason in principle why a suit for negligence could not be brought where teachers failed to take reasonable steps to redress students' underachievement.

> If it comes to the attention of the headmaster that a pupil is underperforming, he does owe a duty to take such steps as a reasonable teacher would consider appropriate to try to deal with such under-performance. To hold that in such circumstances the head teacher could properly ignore the matter and make no attempt to deal with it would fly in the face not only of society's expectations of what a school will provide but also in the fine traditions of the teaching profession itself.[25]

Although the House of Lords seems to have recognized the kind of duty of care rejected by US and Canadian courts, it is

---

[22] *X and others (minors) v. Bedfordshire County Council; M (a minor) and another v. Newham London Borough Council and others; E (a minor) v. Dorset County Council; and other apeals*, [1995] 3 All ER 353 (HL).

[23] See J. Holloway, "The Liability of the Local Education Authority to Pupils Who Receive a Defective Education" (1995-96), 7 *Education and Law Journal* 95, at 97.

[24] *Christmas v. Hampshire County Council*, [1995] NLOR no. 75 (HL).

[25] Ibid., at 395.

unclear how wide its application might be. Because *Christmas* dealt specifically with a headmaster's alleged negligence in not referring a student with learning problems either for a formal assessment or to an educational psychologist, the duty of care might arguably be restricted to similar cases involving non-referral or negligent referral of special education students, and not extend to a general duty to act non-negligently in each and every aspect of the provision of a child's education. However, depending on a subsequent court's policy disposition, the latter is not an impossible interpretation. Even so, all the difficult—if not impossible—problems of proof (especially of causation) demonstrated in the US cases would still need to be overcome by a plaintiff.

Professional Responsibility

The cautious approach of the courts to claims of educational malpractice has received scholarly criticism.[26] It seems logical that the courts could be used as a means of promoting educational competence. It is true that primary responsibility should rest with school boards and the legislatures, but it is desirable to have a judicial check for extreme cases. Moreover, if damages are suffered through malpractice, courts are the bodies charged with the authority and responsibility to order compensation. Problems of proof will ensure that successful malpractice claims against teachers or school boards will be rare. As the US cases show, the causal link between a person's present status and his or her inadequate education is difficult to prove. There are many possible intervening causes apart from the schools, such as broken homes, child abuse, or even an overdose of television. These practical problems, coupled with the high costs of litigation and the general reluctance of Canadians to sue, suggest that there will not be a flood of educational malpractice cases, even if such a cause of action were recognized by the Canadian courts. The floodgates of litigation simply are not likely to be opened.

However, teachers and school boards should accept the challenge of professionalism and admit to the possibility of a malpractice action. Indeed, teachers' organizations and school board associations should take the lead in defining the elements of competent teaching from the educational perspective. It is a difficult

---

[26] J. Cohen, "The ABC's of Duty: Educational Malpractice and the Functionally Illiterate Student" (1977), 8 *Golden Gate University Law Review* 293, is just one example. See also Foster, *supra* note 2.

task but failure may mean leaving the courts to undertake it. Moreover, as outcomes-based education predicated on measurable achievement expected of all children becomes the norm in provincial and local educational policies, the courts may find it easier, as a matter of public policy, to rationalize legal liability when stated outcomes that explicitly or implicitly define a minimally acceptable education are not realized.

At present the courts have developed legal criteria for educational competence on a case-by-case basis.[27] However, the cases are those concerned with physical injuries rather than genuine professional malpractice. Teachers and boards can also take comfort in the supportive approach of courts; there is nothing to indicate that courts will be quick to find educational malpractice on the facts of a particular case. Teachers, like doctors and lawyers, should set their own standards of competence, which can then be considered by the courts as one factor in establishing legal criteria for competent teaching.[28] Quite apart from legal issues, setting standards of competence will force teachers to think more clearly about their jobs; the ultimate beneficiaries will be the students, for whose benefit the educational process exists.

Finally, the topic of educational malpractice needs to be considered beyond the level of the classroom and the individual plaintiff. It also needs to be examined systemically, because it is a problem interwoven with important social equity issues. One might reasonably posit that educational malpractice is more likely to occur in school settings serving disadvantaged students, whether they are economically deprived, culturally different, or physically or mentally challenged. In the first instance, the school district may be relatively "tax poor" and unable to deploy the same resources as richer districts. In the case of children of recent immigrants and First Nations peoples, boards may be unwilling or unable to provide the courses, programs, and special support necessary to afford them true equality of educational opportunity.[29]

Certainly, constitutionally based arguments can be mounted to challenge discriminatory practices in the provision of education.

---

[27] Y.M. Martin and A.C. Nicholls, "Teacher Competence—Emerging Legal Criteria" (1983), vol. 3, no. 6 *Canadian School Executive* 20. The existing legal criteria have been based on liability for physical injuries.

[28] Some steps in this direction have already been taken, such as codes of ethics developed by teachers' unions. However, these are too general to be very helpful.

[29] See J. Paquette, "Rewriting the Social Contract of Ontario Education" (1990), 2 *Education and Law Journal* 243.

It is possible, for example, that s. 15(1) equality rights under the Canadian Charter of Rights and Freedoms[30] might be invoked by students and their parents in assessment-poor school districts to claim that a lower per pupil expenditure on education, compared with richer boards, amounts to a denial of equal benefit of the law.[31] Section 15(1) challenges by physically and mentally disabled pupils seeking to be educated in an integrated class have met with mixed success.[32]

The question that must ultimately be asked and decided regarding educational malpractice is, What should be the role of the law and the courts in promoting the accountability of politicians and educators for the provision of a high standard of education for *all* children? To date, whether they have felt ill-disposed or ill-equipped, the courts in Canada, the United States, and elsewhere have habitually declined to assume such a role. If education is, indeed, the most important of the modern democratic state's social enterprises, as Warren CJ stated so pointedly in *Brown v. Board of Education*[33] more than 40 years ago, it is difficult to fathom a judicial attitude that has so staunchly refused educational malpractice claimants the opportunity of getting even a foot through the courtroom door.

---

[30] Canadian Charter of Rights and Freedoms, part I of the Constitution Act, 1982, being schedule B of the Canada Act, 1982 (UK), 1982, c. 11 (herein referred to as "the Charter").

[31] For an analysis of the possible use of s. 15 of the Charter to challenge the inequity of provincial funding schemes, see J. Oesch, "School Board Financial Equity in Ontario: 1988 and 1989" (unpublished M Ed dissertation, University of Western Ontario, London, 1992), 119-45.

[32] See *Eaton v. Brant (County) Board of Education* (1997), 142 DLR (4th) 385 (SCC).

[33] *Brown v. Board of Education,* 347 US 483; SC 686 (1954).

Index

damages, in general 6

dangerous activities 31-34
 laboratories 33
 physical education 39-40
 vocational classes 32-33

dangerous objects 30-31
 and occupier's liability 77
 effect on standard of care 30-31
 inherently versus potentially
  dangerous objects 30-31, 77

defences, *see* contributory
 negligence; liability, limitation of;
 voluntary assumption of risk

drugs, administration of legal, *see*
 medical treatment

duty
 of parents, *see* parents
 of pupils, to go home after
  school 29
 of school boards, *see* school board
 of supervision before and after
  school 26-30
 of teachers, *see* teachers
 statutory, effect of breach 3, 5,
  52, 109-11
 to protect versus duty to foster
  self-reliance, responsibility
  14-17, 36

duty of care, *see* negligence

educational malpractice 103-113
 advice by counsellors,
  psychologists 111-12
 application of contract law 105
 classification, negligent
  identification, placement of
  exceptional pupils 106-8,
  111-12
 continuing potential for
  liability 110-12
 duty to place pupil in special
  class 107
 failure to educate 105-6, 109-10
 grounds of liability 103-4
 misrepresentation 105
 professional
  responsibility 112-13
 reasons for failure of suits 106,
  108-10

relationship to systemic
 problems 113-14
right to basic education 108
role of courts 114

emergencies, *see also* medical
 treatment 44-46

equality of educational opportunity,
 and educational malpractice 114

exceptional pupils
 and equality of educational
  opportunity 114
 classification, negligent
  identification, placement
  of 106-8, 111-12
 duty of care toward 33
 duty to place in special
  class 107
 tort liability of 94

extracurricular activities, *see*
 accidents; field trips

field trips, *see also* permission
 forms
 board authorization 68-69
 increased risks, effect on
  standard of care 66-67
 mandatory versus optional
  activities 68
 parental permission, 69-71

first aid, *see* medical treatment

foreseeability
 of injury to escaping
  students 42
 of precise type of accident or
  injury 22
 in general 3-5
 probability versus "real" risk 22

guidance counsellors and school
 psychologists' liability for
 negligence 48, 111-12

hallways, duty to supervise 23-24

injury, required for liability 6

in loco parentis, doctrine of 9

invitee, *see* occupier's liability